Resident Evil

Resident Evil

Philip J Reed

Boss Fight Books
Los Angeles, CA
bossfightbooks.com

ISBN 13: 978-1-940535-25-8
First Printing: 2020

Series Editor: Gabe Durham
Associate Editor: Michael P. Williams
Book Design by Cory Schmitz
Page Design by Lori Colbeck & Christopher Moyer

CONTENTS

FOREWORD

Greetings from Tromaville to all "Resident Evil Rapscallions." Toxie and I are honored to introduce a fantastic, #fantoxic book about a major cultural phenomenon in America. Even though I'm more of an expert at making money-losing movies than I am at playing brilliant video games, I know you will emerge from this journey with a greater appreciation of not only *Resident Evil*, but of American pop culture itself.

Over the course of nearly five decades, Troma Entertainment, like *Resident Evil*, has been synonymous with horror—specifically B-movie horror, comedic satire, and gruesome, over-the-top debauchery. In other words, everything that makes a video game or film worth experiencing.

To this day, the motion picture industry's crowning horror achievement remains the 1931 classic *Frankenstein*. This dark, amusing, yet oddly moving masterpiece of horror is the spiritual predecessor to Troma's own *The Toxic Avenger*. And while *Frankenstein* was birthed from the financial success of *Dracula*, *The Toxic Avenger* was a shout-out to Frankenstein's monster. It was also conceived after having read an article in *Variety* predicting the death of the horror genre. I don't think I need to tell you that some things never die, especially when they're told to.

I have written, directed, produced, distributed, and even appeared (notice how I didn't say "acted") in a vast array of independent horror films, and my fellow constituents and I radiate with a passion that only ignites at the opportunity to create "Art." On the set of *Return to Nuke 'Em High*, Team Troma, along with approximately 80 fans from around the globe, soldiered on through long hours. We slept on the floor, ate cheese sandwiches three times a day, and learned to defecate into a paper bag so we could make real, reel independent art.

I don't know what the makers of *Resident Evil* wanted players to take away from the experience, but I admire their dedication to the horrific, to the disgusting, to the grossly disturbing. The fact that parents and politicians hated it is proof that it was doing something right. Kids who grew up playing *Resident Evil* still love it, even though their clearest memories are of the game scaring the hell out of them. That's something horror does well: It repulses you, but it also draws you back in.

People often compare the quality of *Resident Evil* to a B-movie. I think that's high praise. B-movies are fun.

You've probably forgotten more mainstream so-called "A-movies" than B-movies. B-movies stick with you. Sometimes a B-movie even loops around to become a great movie, and it's a thrilling, fantastic experience when that happens. The bad acting and weak story in *Resident Evil* didn't make the experience any less scary. If anything, it might have gotten players to pay more attention to it, to draw closer, unaware of the zombie licking his lips just around the corner.

Audiences might laugh or cringe in the moment, but that doesn't mean they won't have nightmares later. Independent cinema isn't about perfection, it's about making your own damn movie and making it accessible to the public, no matter the size of the audience. There is enough homogenized and sterile content put forth by the conglomerates to make you forget that you can think for yourself.

Horror is good for you. It's entertaining. It's cathartic. Left unchecked, it's easy for your brain to take itself too seriously. But it's important to scare the living daylights out of it now and then. It's important to gross it out. It's important to make sure it's paying attention. A little bit of gore in your entertainment diet is good for you. The world holds enough real horror for us all. Embrace the ridiculous horror games and movies. They are an important escape.

Dear reader, you are holding in your hand a roadmap to and deconstruction of a major cultural icon. Enjoy it, and BE SCARED!!

Lloyd Kaufman

President of Troma Entertainment,
Creator of the Toxic Avenger

The audience is like a giant organ [...]. At one moment we play this note on them and get this reaction, and then we play that chord and they react that way.

And someday we won't even have to make a movie—there'll be electrodes planted in their brains, and we'll just press different buttons and they'll go "oooh" and "aaaah" and we'll frighten them and make them laugh.

Won't that be wonderful?

— Alfred Hitchcock, 1958

BEWARE:
CHILDREN AT PLAY

IT WAS A FRIDAY NIGHT IN 1997. I was sixteen years old. My friend Dave had come over, and there was nothing strange about that. We were both misfits in our tiny town. We each had niche interests that only rarely overlapped, but we bonded over a shared sense of humor and the knowledge that every day that passed got us 24 hours closer to escaping New Jersey.

Dave had mental health problems. I did too. At the time, neither of us knew it. We were both prone to social anxiety and depression, whether or not those were terms we'd have applied to ourselves or each other. I had it bad. Dave had it worse. It would cause him to drop out of high school the following year.

My friend Michael had also come over, and that was a bit strange.

Michael more easily inhabited the larger social world than either Dave or I. He was a good-looking kid with a great shock of blonde hair. He worked summers

7

as a lifeguard, enjoyed crowds, and exercised of his own free will. It was like being friends with a space alien.

Michael brought over the PlayStation that he'd gotten for Christmas, along with his copy of *Resident Evil.*

The game was still fairly new—it was released in both Japan and North America in March 1996—but already its reputation preceded it: *Resident Evil* was violent. It was gory. It was the scariest goddamned thing that had ever been pressed to disc.

At least, that's what I had heard from others who had been brave enough to play it. That reputation looked like it was confirmed by the cover, on which a man with a firearm is about to be overwhelmed by shadowy creatures. I wasn't quite sure what the expression on his face meant. I assumed it was panic. It certainly wasn't confidence.

I honestly wasn't all that interested in playing it, but I didn't want to be the wimp who suggested something else.

It was my first experience with Sony's console. I had owned Nintendo systems exclusively, and while I experienced a sting of jealousy the first time I played *Sonic the Hedgehog* (and another, much deeper sting when I played its sequel), I'd always been happy with the side I'd taken in the console wars. Nintendo games were fun. They had catchy music. They contained adorable, charming worlds to run around in.

From the moment it growled its own title at us, I knew *Resident Evil* was immediately, urgently unlike anything else I had played. I wasn't sure I was up to its challenge. I wasn't familiar with the controller. And, well… I didn't even like horror.

It feels strange to me now, as someone who studies and writes about horror regularly, enthusiastically, lovingly, but back then I couldn't see the appeal in watching killers stalk their victims, monsters pop out of closets, or anything else I assumed happened in those films. Walking through the aisles of Hometown Video, I'd pass by the horror section, its VHS boxes all loose eyeballs and puddles of blood and sinister skulls, being stared at by evil snowmen, evil puppets, evil dentists, trying to avoid looking at them directly lest even the box art give me nightmares.

Who would ever want to watch those things?

The game began with a live-action introduction, looking so much like those video rentals I'd worked so hard to avoid. The action took place in the near future— July 1998. The narration spoke of mysterious, violent murders ending in cannibalism. Onscreen newspaper articles documented the atrocities, reinforcing the truth of what we were being told. The game was already tearing down the wall that separated us from the fiction of what we were about to see. In retrospect, I can see parallels here to everything from the barely-glimpsed crime scene photos of 1974's *The Texas Chainsaw Massacre* to the viral marketing that positioned 1999's *The Blair Witch Project* as genuine footage. At the time, however, all I knew was that the game presenting its own supporting documentation made it even more realistically terrifying.

The intro showed a helicopter setting down in a field, dropping off our heroes to investigate the murders and the disappearance of their colleagues who set out ahead of them. We were introduced to them one by one. One of them, Albert Wesker, looked a hell of a lot like Michael, and Dave and I joked about it.

We played in the dark. It wasn't a conscious decision, but it was fitting. We passed the controller around, and, to be completely honest, the game was more fun to watch than to play. The controls were terrible. The writing and performances—even to a bunch of dumb teenagers—were clearly ridiculous. The game seemed like it was designed poorly at the most basic levels, with camera angles obscuring important details and making it impossible to see what we were doing. Puzzles were inscrutable. Resources were mercilessly limited. The combat was difficult to the point of feeling torturous.

But something kept us playing. Mario drew us in with bright colors and bouncy tunes. Zelda drew us in with gradual empowerment and limitless adventure.

Tetris drew us in with the promise that we could do a little bit better each time.

Resident Evil drew us in by shoving us down and daring us to get back up.

However unfair, however punishing, however cruel the game was, we always did get back up. Michael, Dave, and I wrestled with every obstacle the game put in our path, nearly always unsuccessfully. We struggled like hell to survive the Spencer Mansion.

"This is a masterpiece," I said at the time, to nobody in particular, speaking a basic truth into the night. "It's like nothing I've ever played before."

Actually, wait. My mistake.

What I said was: "Isn't this just *Alone in the Dark*?"

AT MIDNIGHT I'LL
TAKE YOUR SOUL

THE GAME BEGINS BY OFFERING ME a choice between two protagonists, one male and one female. The adventure is confined almost entirely to a creepy mansion infested with zombies and doglike abominations. I have no control over the camera, which is fixed to a set of predetermined angles, only showing me what some invisible director wants me to see.

I struggle to get the hang of what we will eventually call "tank controls," with Up always moving the character in the direction they are facing and Left and Right rotating them in place. I'm still not used to the controls when I encounter my first enemy, which is alarmingly durable and soaks up my ammunition easily.

I survive the fight, but only barely. The game has made it immediately clear that ammunition and health are going to be deeply valuable commodities.

The game, of course, is *Alone in the Dark*.

Alone in the Dark was released in 1992 for MS-DOS. This was four years before *Resident Evil*, and understanding the latter requires a familiarity with the former, which can charitably be described as *Resident Evil*'s inspiration and more honestly described as its cannibalized victim.

In *AitD*, you explore the spooky Hartwood Mansion as either Edward Carnby or Emily Hartwood. The mansion's owner died by his own hand; it's up to you to figure out why and, hopefully, make it out alive.

As in *Resident Evil*, you progress by solving cryptic puzzles, many of which will kill you if solved incorrectly. Ammunition and health are rationed severely. Strict inventory limitations prevent you from carrying everything you find. You piece the story together by reading notes and journals, learning that works of unspeakable evil have been conducted in a secret area beneath the mansion. Monsters outside the front door prevent you from doing the sensible thing and going the hell home.

That's a far-from-complete list of similarities, and more suspicious are the direct lifts of setpieces. Both games hide crucial items in small cubbies behind grandfather clocks, use false books as keys, and feature an early scare in which doglike creatures crash through a window.

As a writer, I'm bothered by creative thievery. Making art is difficult. Whether you write or paint or make video games, inspiration doesn't come on command. There's a lot of waiting. A lot of considering. A lot of struggling to find the best way to convey an idea. A lot of tinkering and revising. Creating something is hard work. Swiping somebody else's idea is not.

AitD was directed and programmed by French developer Frédéric Raynal. I first played it on a demo unit at Discount Computer Warehouse in Tuckerton, New Jersey. I lived close enough that I could walk there, and I did so often. I was twelve at the time. I had very little money. I'd buy gaming magazines and long for titles and systems I knew I'd never be able to afford.

The store was owned by Art, my personal Willy Wonka of discount computing. Art taught me how to cheat in *Minesweeper*.[1] He introduced me to Commander Keen. He showed me "Johnny Castaway," a screensaver featuring a shipwrecked cartoon who could never get off his tiny island. I loved it all.

It was Art who sat me down to play *AitD*. It may have been a sales pitch—and you bet your ass I bought the game—but it didn't feel like one. As soon as I had control of my character, Art told me to push an old trunk onto a trap door. I did so, and was rewarded with the pounding sound of some nasty creature I was glad I didn't have to see, trying to force its way up from below.

---

1 X, Y, Z, Z, Y, Enter, Shift.

This was the first room of the game, and already my heart was in my throat. My mouth was dry. It was (for real this time) like nothing I had ever played before. I was impressed that a game could be so scary.

It's an experience most gamers will have had at some point, only they are far more likely to have had it with *Resident Evil*.

Shinji Mikami, the director of *Resident Evil*, is often seen as the guiding hand behind the franchise. It's a reputation cemented by the fact that he also directed two more of the best-loved titles in the series: the GameCube *Resident Evil* remake and *Resident Evil 4*.

Usually, when discussing *Resident Evil*'s inspirations, Mikami cites an earlier Capcom release: the 1989 Famicom role-playing game *Sweet Home*, an adaptation of a Japanese horror film of the same name.

In an interview with Metro.co.uk, he discussed the direct guidance he received from his boss, Tokuro Fujiwara. "He ordered me to use the *Sweet Home* mechanics and apply them to something else, to make a horror game," Mikami said.

There are valid reasons for Mikami to acknowledge similarities between two Capcom games rather than between one of Capcom's and one by another developer. For instance, citing Raynal's game as *Resident Evil*'s foundation would have likely meant paying him.

Playing *AitD* is all it takes to reveal Mikami's true inspiration, although his earliest acknowledgement seems to be in an interview published in 2014, eighteen years after *Resident Evil*'s release.

"When Sony announced the technical features and the number of 3D elements that could be displayed on the screen, we were skeptical," Mikami said. "That's when I played *Alone in the Dark*, which consisted of fixed sets. It was very interesting because it felt more expressive. The next step was to adapt *Resident Evil* to this model."

The article states that the nascent *Resident Evil* became "a zombie reinterpretation" of *AitD*, without which, Mikami said, "*Resident Evil* would have probably been a first-person shooter." That is a profound artistic debt.

Art has a long history of borrowing from itself, and artists build upon existing works regularly. Stories are recycled. Character types are repeated so that we know who to admire, who to distrust, who to turn to for comic relief. Entire genres hinge upon sturdy adherence to established formulas, such as detective fiction and comedies of manners.

It's bad form, however, to take somebody else's work, make superficial changes, and pass it off as your own. To put it into words any student has heard hundreds of times, you need to cite your sources.

Though at the time I felt as though I were playing the most elaborate example of plagiarism I'd ever seen, I can see clearly now that even if *Resident Evil* borrowed a little too much from *AitD*, it also improved upon it.

Resident Evil and *AitD* used the same ingredients, but, ultimately, it's difficult to argue that Capcom didn't create the superior dish.

It's just a shame they waited eighteen years to thank Raynal for the recipe.

SPLATTER UNIVERSITY

I ENJOYED *ALONE IN THE DARK*, but I never felt compelled to finish it. It was an early dalliance with horror that for me didn't lead to any larger or lasting interest in the genre. It didn't even lead to lasting interest in the game itself.

Resident Evil, by contrast, taught me what horror *was*. It laid the groundwork for my lifelong appreciation of a genre I thought had nothing to offer me.

Resident Evil opens with masterfully efficient chaos. In the brief introductory video, we learn that a police unit called the Special Tactics and Rescue Service (STARS) is investigating a series of cannibalistic murders. It's July 24, 1998, and STARS Alpha arrives at Raccoon Forest to search for the Bravo team, which disappeared shortly after the start of the mission.

No sooner does the helicopter carrying your six-person team touch down than one member is eaten by dogs, Brad the pilot takes off in a panic, and the four stranded remnants—Chris, Jill, Barry, and Wesker—take desperate shelter in the nearby Spencer Mansion.

By the time they make it inside, another member has vanished as well (Chris if you play as Jill, Barry if you play as Chris).

It's a decidedly tense start that sees half the team torn away before you're even given control of your character. If there's strength in numbers, *Resident Evil* opens by making you much weaker.

I've played through the game several times with each character, but I nearly always play as machine expert Jill Valentine.[2] In fact, I'm pretty sure everybody nearly always plays as Jill.

In *AitD*, the choice between Edward and Emily is purely aesthetic. In *Resident Evil*, the choice affects both gameplay and story. Chris is stronger and can absorb more damage; Jill gets a lockpick and has more inventory space. Chris meets up with medic Rebecca Chambers as his supporting character; Jill gets weapons specialist Barry Burton.

As Jill, I step into the eerily empty mansion, hearing nothing beyond the echoes of my boots against the marble floor. Barry and mission leader Albert Wesker are the only other confirmed survivors, and the position of the camera high above makes us appear small and helpless.

---

2 Titles taken from the game's manual.

The characters take a moment to discuss the situation. It's a brief exchange, during which the camera angle changes six times in Jill's version and seven in Chris's. The angle doesn't change to draw attention to an item or the path forward, but to cut to different characters and frame them interestingly as they interact. In the purest sense of the word, it's cinematic.

Admittedly, the conversation itself is less effective than its presentation, with the voice actors delivering their lines so woozily that it seems as though they split a bottle of cough syrup before stepping into the recording booth.

BARRY: What is this?

WESKER: Wow. Whatta mansion!

JILL: *[eight seconds of silence]* Captain Wesker, where's Chris?

A gunshot rings out. The characters turn toward the sound. It's easy to imagine the storyboards and stage directions that brought this sequence to life. Playing older games, we might have been able to imagine lines of code or design documents. But this… this is *directed*.

Even more impressive, though, is the fact that *Resident Evil* doesn't abandon its cinematic approach when you gain control of the character.

Traditionally, cinematic moments in video games were necessarily isolated. In 1988's *Ninja Gaiden*, for instance, the stylish, carefully blocked cutscenes are great, but they are never in danger of being confused with the basic left-to-right platforming of the actual gameplay.

Here, though, with the exception of very few pre-rendered moments, the only visual difference between the game and its cutscenes is a subtle letterboxing effect. The actual game flows into and out of its cutscenes without interruption, as though an unseen director is working in real time to frame shots, switching carefully between camera angles as you cross a room.

Throughout *Resident Evil*, Mikami films his characters with love and care. He stages big moments so they will have maximum impact. He dictates where you—participant and audience—will focus your attention.

Barry tags along with me into the dining room, where he stops to investigate some blood. A grandfather clock ticks the seconds away, amplified and unnerving against the dead silence.

This is the first room in which I have control of Jill, and it's where players truly feel the oppressive (and deliberate) claustrophobia of the fixed camera angles. This is our chance to learn the controls, to become comfortable with driving our character like a vehicle through cramped spaces. It's worth taking the time to familiarize ourselves now, while it's safe.

If we return to the foyer, Wesker orders us to continue the investigation, so we have no choice but to pass through the dining room alone. I do so and find myself in a hallway. Mikami's camera peers down at me from above, showing almost nothing of the hall I'm standing in or where it leads.

Heading north, we find nothing but locked doors. Heading south, though, we encounter the first enemy of the game: the corner.

Often *Resident Evil* will use our inability to see around corners against us. It's a way of making us advance carefully, of encouraging us to think ahead, of keeping us on our toes.

Mikami assumes control and pushes his camera in on a grotesque tableau. A man with ashen skin—and a natty sport coat—is hunched over, chewing wetly on something we can't quite see. Maybe it's a dead body. It's hard to tell. It's dark. Blood soaks the throw rug as the man rips something free from the carcass. And then we get a rare moment of prerendered horror.

He becomes aware of our presence.

He turns slowly.

Deliberately.

It may be a man, but it's also a monster.

Its gaze is still. Unwavering.

It does not panic.

We do.

That image of the rotting zombie in half-turn is hideous, threatening, and genuinely scary. This is a creature that you witness consuming a human corpse like a rack of ribs, and you regain clunky, unready control of your character just in time for it to rise to its feet and step toward you.

Alfred Hitchcock was a master of the iconic, terrifying image. You get the sense when you watch his best movies that he already knew—sitting in the director's chair, filming his actors—exactly what was going to resonate with audiences most. The crop duster bearing down on Cary Grant in *North by Northwest*. Jimmy Stewart hanging by his fingertips in *Vertigo*. Tippi Hedren smoking a cigarette as crows mass quietly behind her in *The Birds*. Hitchcock didn't just direct: He composed visual touchstones that elevated suspense to the status of art.

The zombie's half-turn is one of gaming's greatest Hitchcockian images, and it cements what you might have only suspected before this: You aren't playing a horror game. You are starring in a horror film.

You have two options when it comes to dealing with this zombie: You can fight it, or you can retreat into the dining room. I do the latter and find Barry there, still staring at the puddle of blood, trying, I guess, to intimidate it into talking. He shoots the zombie for me. Barry doesn't need the ammo. I do.

This is an early example of *Resident Evil*'s willingness to adapt and respond to a player's decisions, separating it from something like 2013's *Outlast*, a cinematic horror game that relies on players following one correct path and not accounting for or allowing significant deviation. *Resident Evil*'s horror movie experience doesn't involve yelling "Cut!" when the player goes off-script. Instead, it follows that player and rewrites itself as necessary.

First-time players are unlikely to retreat. This is where *Resident Evil* should be teaching us how to fight. This is the game's first misdirection.

I have no way of remembering how many shots it took to bring this zombie down the first time I played. I wasn't counting; I was too busy flailing and screaming as Michael tried—through laughter—to explain to me how to open my inventory, equip my weapon, and enter a firing stance.

Then, of course, I had to aim—as in physically rotate my character—at the zombie, which felt impossible in a fixed 3D environment. Only then could I finally pull the trigger and miss the monster completely. The zombie grabbed me and bit gory chunks right out of my neck. Michael could barely talk, he was laughing so hard.

This is, again, the first enemy in the game.

Even if you can rely on your shots to connect, the zombie takes around five to seven shots to bring down. That's a good portion of the fifteen bullets Jill starts the game with. Exactly how many shots he'll take is determined by the game's random number generator, which decides both the strength of your attacks and the health of the enemies. Ultimately, you learn your lesson. You may have thought fifteen bullets could kill fifteen enemies, but you'd be lucky to take down two.

If you don't remember having to rotate your character to aim, you were playing a different version of *Resident Evil*. The original Japanese release, under the title *Biohazard*, featured lock-on for firearms: Enter a firing stance and you automatically aim at the nearest enemy. This feature was removed for *Resident Evil*'s Western release, but it was restored in 1997's *Resident Evil: Director's Cut* and 1998's inelegantly named *Resident Evil: Director's Cut Dual Shock Ver.*

The lack of lock-on in itself made *Resident Evil* a significantly tougher game than *Biohazard*, but Capcom didn't stop there. *Resident Evil* increased the health of enemies, decreased the health of the protagonists, reduced the amount of ammunition in the game and, perhaps most cruelly, removed a number of the ink ribbons, which are required to save progress. *Biohazard* was no walk in the park, but *Resident Evil* was a march through Hell.

My first time playing, I checked my health after this battle and saw a red electrocardiogram over the word "danger." Seeing my health represented by an ECG after the game gave me the closest thing I'd ever had to a heart attack felt like outright mockery.

That encounter taught me that fighting wouldn't often be worth it. I'd come out the other side poorer in ammunition and health, and the enemies didn't drop anything to replenish them. Too much fighting could leave you completely defenseless. Investigate the corpse the zombie was eating and you'll learn that it's Kenneth Sullivan, Bravo's field scout. It might also be you if you don't get your shit together.

Like many other games, *Resident Evil* set a baseline feeling of helplessness so that it could eventually empower you. Consider 1986's *Metroid*, which starts you off weak and fragile but rewards exploration with better weapons and health upgrades, or 1998's *Half-Life*, which begins with you swatting aliens with a crowbar and ends with you bringing a military-grade arsenal (and some futuristic sci-fi weaponry to boot) across dimensions to crush the invaders at their source.

Heroes tend to get stronger and better-equipped as their games unfold. From both a design and gameplay standpoint, this makes sense: Gradual empowerment provides a sense of progression. It allows the game to introduce more complex ideas and enemies as it continues, and it allows the player to feel as though they aren't beating endlessly against the same obstacles.

This kind of game design, however, leads to action. To adventure. To triumph.

It does not lead to horror.

Parasite Eve, Square's 1998 classic, has a lot in common with *Resident Evil*: limited inventory, fixed camera angles, horror-movie template, female cop protagonist. Its respawning enemies drop health and ammunition, however, which leads to farming. I enjoyed that game quite a lot, but I never felt scared. The fact that I could always count on enemies dropping items meant I never worried about running out, which did a lot to dilute the horror. *Parasite Eve* is a horror game that, through one design decision, became an action game instead.[3]

Resident Evil takes a different view of empowerment. There's no way to increase your maximum health. You can't upgrade your weapons. You don't unlock more inventory space. Baddies don't drop goodies. You start

---

3 *Resident Evil 4* introduced the same tweak to this series in 2005. If you're really trying to nail down the difference between survival horror and action horror, this is where you should focus your attention. It's Resident Evil reenacting the shift from *Alien* to *Aliens*.

the game as a large, clumsy target, and that's exactly how you'll end it.

Instead, *Resident Evil* opts for psychological empowerment. It doesn't want you taking down every enemy. It doesn't even want you engaging with every enemy. It wants to scare you, but it also forces you to confront and push through the fear.

You learn to stay alert rather than afraid.

You learn to not fire blindly.

You learn which enemies to avoid entirely.

You learn to get used to low-health warnings.

Resident Evil is designed to make you panic, but it teaches you not to. If you do, you will die.

That first zombie's one hell of a teacher, isn't he?

SMILE BEFORE DEATH

JILL AND BARRY RETURN to the main hall to find that Wesker is now missing, too. Their brief search for him turns up no clues, which isn't surprising as it involves Barry yelling Wesker's name exactly once and Jill running in a circle.

If you play as Chris, you're completely alone at this point. If you're Jill, though, you get to discuss the situation with Barry, both characters speaking as if they've just suffered moderate head injuries.

> JILL: Now it's Wesker's time to disappear. I don't know what's going on!
>
> BARRY: Well, it can't be helped. Let's search for him separately. I'll check the dining room again.
>
> JILL: Okay. I'll try the door… on the opposite side.

I genuinely have no idea how Barry thinks Wesker could have entered the dining room as they were stepping out of it, but this exchange is more or less par for *Resident Evil*'s course.

It's been suggested in recent years that *Resident Evil* featured deliberately poor acting and writing as a way of paying homage to B-movies, and that's a nice thought. Wouldn't it be great if Capcom were embracing its love of cheesy horror along with us?

Believing that, however, requires us to ignore the fact that later games—and the remake of this game—took deliberate steps toward better performances, farther from B-movie territory rather than closer to it. We'd also have to ignore the folks who actually made the game.

In the interview with Metro.co.uk, Mikami was asked about *Resident Evil*'s notorious performances. He took responsibility for both the writing and the acting.

"The original script was in, of course, Japanese and someone translated it into English, and I didn't know the quality of the translation," he said.

His limited understanding of the language also informed his direction of the actors.

"When they spoke the dialogue in English it was very fast so I couldn't really follow," he said. "So I asked those actors to speak slower."

Knowing this, the performances in *Resident Evil* make a lot more sense. It was a cast of English speakers having to slowly recite clumsy dialogue so that a Japanese team could understand them.

Of course, understanding the context of these awkward, stilted performances doesn't make them any less funny.

> BARRY: Here's a lockpick. It might be handy if you, the master of unlocking, take it with you.
>
> JILL: Thanks. Maybe I'll need it!

Barry promises her that if anything happens, she can go back to the foyer. "This time," he says, "I'll be there." Which is odd for at least two reasons: Barry isn't the one who disappeared earlier—he's the only supporting character who *hasn't* disappeared—and if you do return, he isn't there.

Part of the reason I'm focusing on Jill is that just about all of the cultural memory of the game comes from her version of events. Certain awkward quotables, such as the above exchange with Barry, Barry rescuing you from a ceiling trap with the observation that you were "almost a Jill sandwich," Barry's voice acting… heck, everything about Barry. These are things you only experience in a Jill run, and they're the things fans remember most fondly.

Several years after he introduced me to *Resident Evil*, Michael and I attended the Richard Stockton College of New Jersey. (It's a university now.)

I was working at an appliance store to put myself through school, selling and delivering home appliances along the Jersey Shore. I finished my days feeling beaten and exhausted. Michael was a lifeguard at a casino. He reminded me often, usually when I was feeling the lowest, that he didn't work hard at all. Most of the time he didn't even pay attention to the pool. That sounded appallingly dangerous to me, which might be why he mentioned it so many times. He wore sunglasses and often napped behind them. He took to wearing them even when he wasn't working, further enhancing his resemblance to Wesker, *Resident Evil*'s secret villain.

The more time I spent with Michael, the less time I spent with Dave. When we did all get together, Michael must have taken some kind of pleasure in pitting Dave and me against each other. It's something I can only recognize in retrospect. Who made more money? Who had the prettier girlfriend? Who was funnier? He'd pose the questions and work out the answers, sometimes exhaustively, while we sat there, simmering, pretending to ignore him but never able to.

I don't think Michael ever really cared about the outcome. He just enjoyed sowing discord between his anxious friends. If we didn't happen to bite, he'd find a new topic. Eventually one would work. My social anxiety kept me from having many friends, and I must have been willing enough to believe that this was just what friendship was like. Instead of recognizing his manipulations and spending less time with him, I started spending less time with Dave. It avoided conflict.

Most of my time with Michael was spent watching bad movies. One holiday break, someone I didn't know gave Michael the key to her dorm room because she needed him to feed her fish. We spent that break renting and marathoning terrible, terrible movies on her very nice television. She left some granola bars behind and I ate them. These were wild years.

We liked good horror movies, too. We watched 1941's *The Wolf Man* and were genuinely impressed by it. We had expected silly fun. What we got was Lon Chaney Jr.'s deeply tragic performance as Larry Talbot, a man turned monster not through hubris or for being a jerk, but for being a good guy. Talbot is bitten while fighting off a defenseless woman's attacker. In any other genre, he'd be lionized. In horror, well… things tend to go differently.

Mainly, though, we liked crap. We stalked video stores and bought a bunch of cheap "50 Horror Classics" DVD sets that didn't contain a single recognizable title.

I don't remember how or why a love of bad movies bonded us, but I do know that I, like so many others, can trace my appreciation to *Mystery Science Theater*

3000, a show that wallowed in the giddy delights of movies whose creators had no idea what they were doing. I started watching the show sometime after Mike Nelson took over as host in 1993. Nelson and his wisecracking robots helped me realize that horror was supposed to be fun. It was supposed to frighten and unnerve you, yes, but it was also entertainment. If the movie you were watching failed to provide that entertainment, well, you and your friends could always make your own fun at its expense.

By the time college rolled around in 1999, I was a big fan of the worst cinema had to offer, and Michael and I dedicated ourselves to unearthing moronic gems. There was 1988's *555*, much of which was filmed on oddly underfurnished sets that made any attempt to suspend disbelief impossible. There was 1965's *Bloody Pit of Horror*, and its scenery-chewing Crimson Executioner became Michael's costume that Halloween. There was 1972's *Three on a Meathook*, which instantly became and remains my favorite bad horror film, not least because the movie opens with exactly four bodies on meathooks.

Resident Evil, however, was not one of our ironic pleasures, and Michael didn't introduce it to me as one. He was fully aware of the weakness of the acting—I distinctly remember him laughing at Barry's delivery of the word "blood" as though it were the funniest thing in the world—but *Resident Evil* didn't become popular because it was corny. It became popular because it was terrifying. As with *The Wolf Man*, you might periodically chuckle at its flaws, but it still managed to hit you hard.

In his 1927 essay "Supernatural Horror in Literature," H.P. Lovecraft discusses Horace Walpole's 1764 novel, *The Castle of Otranto*, which is considered the first Gothic horror novel.

Lovecraft doesn't have many compliments for Walpole's writing. He calls the story "tedious, artificial, and melodramatic," says it's "impaired by a brisk and prosaic style," and sums it up as "flat, stilted, and altogether devoid of the true cosmic horror." And yet: "It was seriously received by the soundest readers and raised in spite of its intrinsic ineptness to a pedestal of lofty importance in literary history."

Lovecraft celebrates the elements that sent shivers down his spine, such as "strange lights, damp trap-doors, extinguished lamps, moldy hidden manuscripts, creaking hinges, shaking arras, and the like." These are all things that went on to become recurring elements of horror in general.

Walpole's novel may not have been great, but it affected its audience deeply in spite of its flaws. "An harmonious milieu for a new school had been found," Lovecraft wrote, "and the writing world was not slow to grasp the opportunity." Today we might say it invented a genre.

Resident Evil's characters may all speak like they moonlight as crash test dummies, but the danger feels real. The atmosphere is effectively stifling. The brooding soundtrack keeps you on edge. You'll laugh at a line delivery one moment, and scream for help that won't come the next.

In 2013, I had the pleasure of seeing RiffTrax, a project fronted by my favorite permutation of the *MST3K* cast: Mike Nelson, Kevin Murphy, and Bill Corbett. In a live setting, they riffed through the entirety of George A. Romero's 1968 masterpiece, *Night of the Living Dead*, one of the greatest and most important B-movies ever made. It was a lot of fun, laughing with strangers in a crowded theater at jokes about a cheesy old horror film.

Then we got to the end.

I'm sure the RiffTrax guys kept telling jokes, and I'm sure they were funny, but there was a universal gasp in the audience when Ben, having alone survived the night's zombie onslaught, was shot dead by a careless posse the next morning.

I'd wager most of the audience hadn't seen the film before. They came out to watch a classic and laugh at some dad jokes. They came neither to pay attention to the film nor to think about it critically, but so potent is *Night of the Living Dead*—and so perfectly cruel is its ending—that Ben's death mattered anyway. It succeeded in spite of its context. It was a strange feeling, witnessing the horror burst through the comedy like a gunshot.

Resident Evil manages to offer both silly fun and genuinely good horror. And, like the best B-movies, it still has the power to fuck us up.

DOGS OF HELL

RESIDENT EVIL KNOWS HOW to structure its scares, and that's good horror direction. You may jump when Jason Voorhees or Freddy Krueger or Michael Myers pops up, but that's not horror. Horror is the knowledge that they *could* pop up at any time.

In discussion with director François Truffaut, Hitchcock outlined a hypothetical scene in which two people have a conversation at a table. There is a bomb under the table, which neither the characters nor the audience know is there until it explodes. "The public is *surprised*," Hitchcock says, but that's about it.

Craft that same scene differently and surprise is replaced by the much more rewarding suspense. This time, Hitchcock shows the audience the bomb before the characters arrive. "The public is *aware* that the bomb is going to explode at one o'clock, and there is a clock in the decor. The public can see that it is a quarter to one," he says. "In these conditions this innocuous conversation becomes fascinating because the public is participating in the scene. The audience is longing to warn the characters on the screen: 'You shouldn't be talking about such trivial matters. There's a bomb beneath you and it's about to explode!'"

He argues that he's given the second audience a more rewarding experience. "In the first case we have given the public fifteen seconds of *surprise* at the moment of the explosion," he says. "In the second case we have provided them with fifteen minutes of *suspense*."

The encounter with the first zombie is *Resident Evil* planting its bomb in plain sight. Yes, it has killed me—more times than I'd care to confess—but it's the game showing the audience what danger looks like, why we'll need to proceed with caution, and the rules for keeping ourselves safe.

The next few screens, quiet as they are, serve as the unbearable space before that bomb detonates. You return to the main hall. Large and imposing, yes, but safe. Then it's time to explore the Spencer Mansion further, and surely your eyes are drawn to the blue door, which seems just out of place enough to be important.

You enter it and find yourself in the exhibition room. It's just as quiet here. Just as safe. It's another chance to learn how to play the game, to get familiar with its controls and atmosphere. There's even a simple task involving finding a way to retrieve a map from the top of a statue, training you on the types of puzzles you can expect to encounter.[4] Thorough explorers can find a hidden enclosure with an injured, crawling zombie, a great way to practice combat with little risk. The atmosphere is completely sedate.

For at least two rooms in a row, then, you're safe. There are no threats. The game rewards slow, methodical exploration and careful attention to detail. It's taking it easy on you.

Then you open the door to the hallway. What you'll find there is…

…nothing.

It's a long, L-shaped room. In contrast to the hallway in which you encountered the first zombie, the camera angle here gives you a complete, unobstructed view of what's ahead.

Which is nothing.

The camera stays at a distance, facing you, revealing almost the entire long hallway ahead. There's nothing hiding here. There's not even anywhere for something to hide. The magician demonstrates that there's nothing up his sleeve.

There are a couple of small cabinets against the wall. You might try investigating them. You won't find

---

4 The game's demo mode shows you how to solve this puzzle if you linger on the title screen long enough, so it's definitely not intended to be a brain buster.

anything if you do. It's just a corridor leading you from one important room to another. Connective tissue. Logistical necessity. There is, quite literally, nothing to see here.

Walk a bit farther down the hallway and the camera shifts to an angle behind you. Now you can see all the way down the hall. Perhaps there's something around the corner, but until that corner, at the very least, you're safe. There's nothing up this sleeve, either.

So you advance, and a dog crashes through the window behind you.

This is unfair. This is not the way the game is supposed to work. Rooms might contain enemies, but they can't suddenly be invaded by enemies out of nowhere. This is a game. Games have rules. You escaped the dogs by entering the mansion. Dogs prevent you from leaving through the front door. These are outside dogs. They aren't allowed in the house.

But this dog doesn't care, smashing the boundary between one part of the game and another in a shower of broken glass, leaving you to deal—*now*—with the repercussions.

The camera foregrounds the dog during its entrance. You might watch it stumble and slide across the floor, forgetting that this isn't a cutscene and you aren't safe. But it darts at you, impossibly quickly, and you'd better hope you know the way around *Resident Evil*'s clunky controls by now because if you don't, you're quite clearly fucked.

You panic. You run.

The dog is fast. It's a small target. Zombies are slow, mindless bricks of meat, and even they put up a fight. What the hell are you supposed to do with this nimble little shit?

At this early point in the game, *Resident Evil* knows you're still getting used to things. That's why the hallway is straight, narrow, and empty. The design of the area ensures that when the dog crashes through the window, you're already moving away from it. You don't have to grapple for a decision; psychological inertia will keep you moving forward. A lot faster now, but still forward, no longer worried about what might be around that corner, because you're focusing on what's definitely right behind you.

And so you turn that corner, and the camera reveals, for a fleeting moment of desperate relief, that there's nothing there waiting for you.

…at which point a second dog crashes through another window up ahead.

Now you're between them. You're trapped in a pincer maneuver. (A Doberman pincer?) The fact that the first dog appeared behind you prevented you from even thinking about going back the way you came. That's fair. We are wired as human beings to run away from—rather than into—danger. But now, with a second dog ahead of you and a narrow corridor restricting your movement, there's nothing else to do; one way or another, you have to proceed into danger.

Try to fumble with your firearm and you'll just chew through your already limited ammunition.[5] You need to move and you need to move *now*.

Resident Evil didn't have to be artful about this sequence. The dogs, which we'll later learn are infected canines called Cerberuses, could have been a cheap jump scare. But jump scares give the audience its fifteen seconds of surprise and no more. *Resident Evil* knows better. It knows that scary isn't scary *enough*.

The developers took the inherent shock of a monster crashing through a window and gave us the most lovingly constructed horror movie sequence that was never actually in a horror movie.

The dogs didn't scare you. Capcom did.

---

5 Admittedly, the Director's Cut and later releases with lock-on make shooting the animals a far more viable option.

THEM!

RESIDENT EVIL'S LOVE FOR and understanding of horror movies is obvious throughout the game, from its choice of camera angles to its enemy design to the gradual unspooling of its plot. Nowhere, though, is it more apparent than in the *actual* horror movie footage that bookends the game.

At some point in production, Mikami and his team decided that they would lean into the decidedly cinematic nature of their game and give players a live-action introduction and conclusion that would introduce them to—and then escort them out of—the game's world. Bookending the game this way is a fascinating decision, and one that few other games—and no other game in this series—even attempted.

As the first thing any new player saw after booting up *Resident Evil*, the live-action sequences are an important part of its history, and I wanted to learn about how, exactly, they came together. To accomplish this, I set about tracking down the stars of *Resident Evil's* miniature horror movie.

This turned out to be rather difficult, as the actors were only credited by their first names. What's more, until recently, none of them knew they were in the game.

"All I recall is my agent telling me that I had an audition, and it was for a video game by Capcom," remembered Charlie Kraslavsky, who played Chris.

Kraslavsky was the first of the actors I managed to find. He's a handsome man, almost strikingly so, something his costars saw fit to mention as well. He was born and raised in Tokyo and now lives in California.

"I never saw the footage until a few years ago," he told me, still in a kind of disbelief. "Someone I used to work for was really into games, and he was like, 'Hey, I think I saw you!' He'd just been surfing on YouTube and he came across it. 'That's Charlie!' He sent me a link and I was so happy, because I'd never seen the footage and I never knew how it had come out." This was in 2012 or 2013, about a decade and a half after the game's release. Kraslavsky only remembered the game by its original Japanese name. "As far as I was concerned, it was just called *Biohazard*," he said.

At the time of shooting, in or around the summer of 1995, Kraslavsky was working for the Inagawa Motoko Office, or IMO, a talent agency in Tokyo that he described as one of the biggest sources of actors and extras for Japanese TV.

"Day to day, we would always be wearing two hats," he said. "We would be calling people, doing casting, taking people to auditions. Because I speak Japanese fluently, I would also be an interpreter. And I'd be an actor. All in the same day."

It was hectic, but it's an experience Kraslavsky remembers fondly.

"It was a really fun time in my life," he said, "those four or five years that I worked for IMO."

Capcom hired IMO to supply all of its onscreen talent for *Resident Evil*, and Kraslavsky got the role of Chris based on his looks alone.

"They pretty much just selected who they wanted from photos," he said. The audition itself was a formality. "It didn't seem like there was anyone else being considered for the part. That was pretty much true for all the parts."

Capcom had concept art and early in-game models for the characters, so IMO only needed to find actors who resembled them. This led to a stroke of luck for Greg Smith.

Unlike Kraslavsky, Smith was not trying to make a living as an actor. An assistant school principal from Australia, he was on loan to Tokyo's education department for one year and just happened to be with a friend who had business at IMO.

"I walked in and a guy said, 'Ahh! You're the one we want,'" Smith told me. "I didn't know what he was talking about. Then he showed me pictures of this guy, who I eventually found out was going to be Barry

Burton. It looked very similar to me. He was tall, he had wide shoulders, he had a red beard and muscles." Smith laughed. "He probably had more muscles, but they built muscles into the clothes."

After filming, Smith didn't think much about the job. "I kind of forgot about it," he said, until one day, back home in Australia, he was stopped by a fan. "This kid said, 'Ahh, you're in a game!' And I said, 'Oh, possibly.' He said, 'Oh, yeah yeah,' and he told me about it. Then I forgot about it for another… 20 years?"

It wasn't until around 2016 that he saw *Resident Evil* for himself.

"My son-in-law said, 'Look! It's really you!'" Smith told me. "And then I actually saw the talking parts for the first time, and I realized that they dubbed my voice. With an American accent."

Before shooting, the cast came together to rehearse, get fitted for their costumes, and decide on any final touches to their appearances.

"I naturally have very dark, almost black hair, but the character was blond," Kraslavsky remembered.[6] "To

---

6 The earliest concept art I've been able to find of Chris Redfield with blond hair is, strangely, for *Resident Evil – Code: Veronica*, released in 2000. Kraslavsky could be slightly misremembering, or there could have been earlier versions of Chris's design that I haven't seen.

dye my hair, they just used peroxide. I was supposed to be blond, but it ended up looking ginger."

With the character designs already settled, the crew had a sturdy template to work from. Even so, there was room for confusion.

"In the beginning they thought they would want me to have stubble, but I remember the stylist and the director having a big difference of opinion about that," Kraslavsky said. "I remember the stylist saying, 'No, he would never have stubble. He's a very disciplined warrior. He would always shave.' And the director said, 'Yeah, but he's out there, he's fighting. He's not always going to have time to shave.'"

Mitsuhisa Hosoki, the director of the game's live-action sequences, won the battle but lost the war.

"They asked me to grow my stubble out, but because my hair is so dark the stubble was very dark and the hair was very gingery," said Kraslavsky. "It didn't match up at all, so the final decision was that I'd be clean shaven."

Chris Redfield, disciplined warrior, canonically found time to shave.

Smith remembers that the first shooting date was about one week later. He arrived at the train station early in the morning and met a representative from IMO. The train took them to a van, which drove them to the outskirts of Tokyo. From there they walked about half a mile to a small building.

"I walked in there and met Charlie and the rest of the group," Smith said. "They dressed us up and did our makeup, and then they shot all the helicopter scenes inside the building."

"I just remember thinking how awesome the costume was," Kraslavsky said. "I'd never seen anything like it."

Though they were shot first, the helicopter scenes were actually used for the game's ending. The actors involved didn't know the purpose of this footage.

"I think it was supposed to be, like, after we battled," Kraslavsky said, "and we're just kind of sitting there, relaxing, and we're all dirty."

He also remembers that the actors assumed their characters were just resting. He wasn't even sure he was told it was meant to take place in a helicopter.

"It was just some kind of office that they had rented, but it was very plain," he said. "It was really cheaply made."

Multiple permutations of this scene were filmed to be used in the game depending upon how certain events played out. For instance, Chris and Rebecca have a conversation, but only if Jill doesn't survive. If both Rebecca and Jill survive, Rebecca naps on a cot while Chris and Jill join hands. If Chris, Jill, and Barry survive, we get the same scene, but with Barry checking the sights on his gun instead of Rebecca sleeping. If Jill and Barry survive without Chris, we get some dialogue between the two of them. If only Jill or only Chris survives, we get a scene of that character sitting silently, the lone survivor of the Spencer Mansion. Oddly, there was no version of the scene filmed in which all four characters survive, though, according to future games, that is the canonical ending.

For this scene, Kraslavsky once again inadvertently pitted Hosoki and the stylist against each other.

"I've taken off all the armor and stuff, and it's just a white tee shirt and I still have the pants and the kneepads on," Kraslavsky said. "And they were like, 'The shirt's too clean,' because it was a brand-new white shirt." He proposed a practical solution. "There was a gravel parking lot outside and it had rained recently, so there were some puddles. I said, 'Well, if you want, I'll just roll around in the parking lot and get it dirty.'"

Kraslavsky spent the next few minutes rolling in wet gravel while the cast and crew waited for him inside. When he returned, the stylist gasped and Kraslavsky was terrified he'd gone too far. Fortunately for him, Hosoki disagreed.

"The director said, 'Go back out there! Roll around some more. Get it more dirty.' So I did! I went back out there and rolled around in the puddles and the gravel and finally, after I did it for a while, he said, 'Okay, that's it.'"

Smith remembers that this is also when they shot an introductory sequence for each character. In the final edit, narrator Ward Sexton recites each character's name as the actor strikes a pose. Smith remembers having lines during this sequence, but they were ultimately not used in the game.

Shooting took up most of the day, and though there was a good deal of downtime, Smith wasn't complaining. "They did feed us reasonably well," he said.

The only major actor not involved in the helicopter scenes was Eric Pirius, who played Wesker.

Pirius, an athletic, handsome man with a chiseled jaw, still resembles his character strongly. He looks as though a pair of sunglasses is all it would take to get him to betray STARS all over again.

Like the others, Pirius was cast from a photo.

"The interesting thing about IMO," Kraslavsky told me, "was that pretty much anyone that was a Westerner or foreign to Japan in general would come there and register. It was known as the place where you'll get to do some work as an extra, and it'll be fun, and you'll make maybe $100 or $150 for a day's work."

He described a core group of actors who were hoping to parlay small parts into larger careers. "We would book them as much as we could," he said, "because we knew they were our regulars and they were trying to make a living at it."

This brought Kraslavsky and Pirius together before *Resident Evil* did.

"Eric was one of our regulars," he said. "I would see him at auditions and odd jobs. We weren't close, but we had a friendship."

Perhaps the knowledge that Chris and Wesker were friends in real life ruins your childhood. I think it enriches mine.

Unlike friendly Kraslavsky or avuncular Smith, Pirius is a man of few words.

"Type A," he said when I asked him to describe himself. "Married. No kids. Oldest of four."

He learned he was in *Resident Evil* around February 2018. I asked him if anybody ever recognizes him as Wesker. He said, "Hell no."

Pirius was born in Red Wing, Minnesota, but didn't live there long. "I grew up in Alaska, attended college at Vassar, and lived in Tokyo for ten years," he told me.

In his spare time, Pirius enjoys mountain biking and races competitively. He prides himself on his creativity, resourcefulness, and determination. I asked him what made him move to Tokyo. He answered, simply, "Sushi and women."

"I made a good living doing on-camera print and video work and voice work for seven years," Pirius said.

He said he knew "zero" about the project before they started shooting.

According to Smith, the second and final shooting session took place at night, about two days after the main shoot. Once again, he was met at a train station and driven to the filming location, this time near a river.

"It was a dryish river with lots of foliage," he told me. "And bulrushes—as we call them in Australia—reeds and all of those things growing out. There was a big van there and that's where we sat and waited to do the shoot. We had another van that we dressed up in and where we'd rehearse."

Here they filmed *Resident Evil*'s opening sequence, during which STARS Alpha lands in a field and is attacked by monsters. The actors didn't quite know what the monsters were supposed to be, and they wouldn't know until they saw the edited footage so many years later.

"If I remember, they described the beasts we were supposed to be fighting as sort of like wolf creatures, like wolfmen," Kraslavsky said. "They might have shown us a sketch, I don't remember, but for the most part we just had to imagine what we were up against."

The crew brought actual dogs to the shoot for the actors to react to, which amuses Smith in retrospect.

"Those dogs!" he laughed. "You know those vicious dogs? They were as friendly as anything. They were beautiful dogs. They'd sit with us and we'd be petting them. All those vicious dogs were really friendly dogs."

The actors were instructed to flee the animals, periodically firing blanks as an off-camera smoke machine chugged away.

"It was hot, muggy, and dark," Pirius remembered. "With the smoke everywhere, it was a little confusing." As best as he can recall, the direction he received was just to run around, "seemingly randomly," and yell.

"It was great fun shooting the guns," Smith said. "Playing cowboys, shooting guns everywhere. It was just so much fun!"

Like many others before me, I attempted to track down the actors who played Jill and Rebecca. Also like them, I failed. I found a number of dead ends and false positives. I chased exciting new leads that led to the same old disproven conclusions.

However, an unexpected breakthrough occurred as this book was being prepared for publication. Fred Fouchet, of the fan blog Raccoon STARS, successfully identified the actor who played Rebecca, who is credited in the game only as Linda. To this day, she prefers to keep her surname unpublished.

As with the rest of the cast, Linda had no idea she was in *Resident Evil*. In February 2019, Fouchet showed her the footage for the first time. "It was so nice to finally get a chance to see it," she told him. "I was really young when I did the shoot and never saw half of my work."

She seems to have only positive memories of the shoot, and remembers the staff being "very kind." That particular job stood out for her because she had almost exclusively been finding work in Japan as a model.

"I went to ten to fifteen casting [calls] every day," she told Fouchet. "There was a casting sheet in the model van. We would drive around from morning 'til dawn every single day, going on auditions. The sheet would be very basic. 10:00 lingerie. 12:00 magazine. 13:00 commercial for Morinaga. There were regular clients and huge cattle calls."

She recalls being on the set for the dog-attack scene, even though her character was not involved. The only scenes Linda needed to shoot were Rebecca's introduction and the two versions of the ending in which she survived.

Linda remembers the animatronic versions of the dogs looking "really lifelike." The fact that there *were* animatronic versions of the dogs might come as a surprise to Western fans, who only ever experienced a censored version of the intro. The original *Biohazard* included a few more seconds of footage in which the animals were shot and their faces gushed blood. The animatronics were used in that practical effect.

Jill's actor, credited in the game only as Inezh, remains unidentified. Based on how recently the others have learned they were in the game, it's likely she doesn't know anybody is looking for her.

Kraslavsky told me Rebecca's and Jill's actors could have been what IMO called "transients." "These were people who, for whatever reason, were in Tokyo for a short time, and they'd come and register," he explained.

"I don't remember a lot about them because they were only there for a short time."

He remembers Inezh actually spelling her name Ines, and that she was young, possibly still in high school.

Smith lost his jovial demeanor when I asked about the female actors. "There was one girl," he said. "She was a bit strange. She was different. Little blonde girl. She was really weird." As far as I am able to tell, he is remembering Inezh, but it's impossible to know for sure. "She should have been home with her mother. She shouldn't have been there. She was traveling in Japan by herself and working as an actress, come whatever. She was only about fifteen or sixteen."

As a professional educator and father of three daughters, Smith wasn't comfortable with her situation.

Assuming that was Inezh, he had a much different memory of Linda. "She was about sixteen or seventeen, but her mother was with her and made sure everything was above board," he said. "Which it was. Even if we weren't professional actors, we had professional directors and everything."

Linda's overriding memory of her costars is how much younger and less experienced she felt in comparison. "I remember them looking like adults compared to me," she said. "I had smaller bones."

Her youthful, Western appearance certainly made her a good match for the sprightly but inexperienced Rebecca. In order to help her better match the character's in-game model, though, they had to dye her hair "some pinkish-brown color."

She also doesn't remember much about Inezh. "I remember she looked like a woman," she said, in contrast to the "girl" she herself felt like. "Pretty, but not model-type."

As little as we know about Inezh, we know even less about the actor who appears briefly as vehicle specialist Joseph Frost, the game's first on-camera death. He's credited only as Jason, and Kraslavsky remembers him as "a tall, geeky kid. Kind of nerdy, awkward, skinny."

With most of the footage for *Resident Evil* in the can, Kraslavsky had one final scene to film in a nearby warehouse.

"There were scenes in a corridor, and we're getting attacked," he said, referring to a short clip that opens the game, in which Chris is stalked and attacked by an unseen creature. "The sequence ends with an eye, and that's my eye. It spreads wide open in terror. If I remember, I was told, 'Alright, you're getting killed now and we're going to do a closeup of your eye. Open your eye in fear, as big as you can open it.' And I think in proportion to my face, my eyes are kind of small to begin with. And they were like, 'Wider! Open it wider!' And I said, 'This is as wide as they go!' They said, 'Okay, put your index fingers above and below your eye, and as we do the closeup, pull it open as wide as you can.' So that's how we did that shot."

The filming ended around five o'clock the next morning.

"Basically, that was the end of it," Smith said. "I asked if I could keep the dog tags that said 'Barry Burton,' and they wouldn't let me. I was after a bit of *omiyage*, which in Japanese means, like, 'a gift from something you've done.' They weren't into that. They said, 'Oh, yeah, we'll look into it.' Of course, that never happened."

Kraslavsky assumed the footage would be split into clips that would play between levels. It was a strange experience for me, a fan, to explain the ultimate use of the footage to the guy who starred in it.

"I had no idea," Kraslavsky said. "Obviously *Resident Evil* is huge. It has a huge following. And I didn't even know I was part of it until five or six years ago. I thought it was just this video game called *Biohazard*. Learning I'm in it was a revelation to me."

Smith echoed the sentiment. "It didn't mean a lot to me at the time," he said. "I would have embraced those three days a lot more. It was only three days of my life and it was really twenty years later that I knew exactly what it was, and what we'd done, and the impact. The amount of people that really liked it."

Linda, though younger, still carries a sense of wistfulness in her description of the experience. "It was a nice job," she said. "The Japanese are generally extremely kind. Being a foreigner—white, blonde, skinny with blue eyes in the 90s—was dreamy. So I felt very happy in Japan. Life was easy."

Kraslavsky was amazed when he started hearing from fans.

"One of them was like, 'That's my Halloween costume every year,'" he said. "I just found it so amazing that I was this character that I had no idea was near and dear to so many people. Other fans are telling me, 'I played the game all the time. You're part of my childhood.' It just floored me."

I asked Pirius his feelings about appearing in *Resident Evil*. Wesker to the bone, he was less effusive. "Fondness," he said. "Why not? It was good times."

"At the time," Smith told me, "it didn't mean a lot to me and I had a lot of other things happening in my life. I was doing lots of stuff, traveling overseas, all those kinds of things, and living a life. I would have tried to get back into it. I've been the original Barry all through life, and I didn't realize it."

I wanted to know if he was aware that Barry was something of a fan-favorite character.

"Yeah, well, he should be!" he replied without missing a beat. "He was a really good guy. Barry was a family man, from what I'd worked out at the time from the script. He loved his family. He was just doing a job, and he had to do it. He was a bit like the old war horse. I was 39 and Barry was the same age as me, so he was like an old soldier.

He'd been around a bit. I could relate to it. He had two daughters, I had three. He had a wife; I had a wife."

His relating to the character extends beyond the bounds of the game. Smith is a proud biker and flies to America to participate in the annual Sturgis Motorcycle Rally. I asked what he rode. "What else would Barry do but ride a Harley?" he replied. "Barry is a Harley kind of guy."

I was surprised that Smith was given information about Barry's backstory, while Pirius said he never even knew Wesker was the game's villain. Of course, Smith had to shoot a version of the helicopter scene in which he opened up about his family to Jill. Pirius, by contrast, filmed no scenes regarding his status as turncoat, so it was information he didn't need.

"When my son-in-law showed me, I thought there might be some more royalties, but I never got any royalties out of it," Smith said, laughing. "I wish I'd been in the rest of the franchise. I might have been a millionaire."

"I had an acting career in my 20s in Tokyo," Kraslavsky reflected. "Maybe 22 to 26. Those four years, that was my acting career in Tokyo. Then I put it behind me and I did a lot of other stuff. And I got back into acting again about ten years ago when I was living in San Francisco. You know, the acting bug kind of reared its head again. But I've never…"

He trailed off.

"There is one other project I did back then, in Tokyo, which was a pretty big part," he said. "I was the villain in a made-for-cable movie. I've done lots of work as an extra, work on commercials, just little bit parts here and there. But *Resident Evil* is probably the most important work I've done."

When fans started getting in touch, Kraslavsky began to wonder.

"This all started kind of bubbling up, and I started to feel like, wow, you know? Maybe there's a chance here," he said. "Let's reboot *Resident Evil* and let's get as many of the original people and just reboot it with them. Maybe they could reboot the movies, maybe I could have a cameo, maybe I could…"

He trailed off once more.

"I kind of put acting on the side now," he said, quieter.

Kraslavsky doesn't have a negative thing to say about anybody. Every time he mentioned a colleague, he made sure to tell me how great they were to work with, how great they were at their jobs, how great it was to be around them. It was only when talking about himself, considering his own legacy, wondering what might have been, that his positivity faltered.

"I'm glad I found out," he told me. "I could have gone through the rest of my life had nobody ever figured out who I was, and I never would have known that I've impacted so many people, and that I'm a character that's near and dear to their hearts. I'm just really, really, really happy to find all this out."

TRAP THEM AND
KILL THEM

Exploring the east wing, I find a door that requires four crests to unlock. It's not a puzzle—the game will automatically put them in the correct slots—but in looking for the crests I find two of the game's most memorable trap rooms.

The first is an art gallery, though the camera is positioned high enough that its downward angle makes it difficult to see the paintings. It does make it pretty easy to see the crows perched above, though…

By foregrounding the crows, our director creates a sense of looming menace. When we do get a lower angle in this room, it's tilted upward to make sure we haven't forgotten them. We're being watched or, perhaps more appropriately, observed.

Switches near each painting let us know there's a puzzle to be solved. The crows periodically screech their warnings from above, letting us know we'd better solve it correctly.

The puzzle isn't all that complex. Guided by the text descriptions of the portraits, we need to hit the switches in sequence from the youngest subject to the oldest. Doing this gets us the Star Crest. Hitting them in the wrong sequence brings the crows down in a whirl of blood and feathers. You can reset the crows by leaving and reentering the room, but unless you have health to spare, it's not a good idea to brute-force the solution. Also, you never have health to spare.

The other trap room, a parlor, is memorable for very different reasons depending upon your choice of protagonist.

Here you find a shotgun hanging on the wall. It's a valuable find, and it might actually let you start doing some real damage to the zombies that have been sopping up your precious ammo. There are no enemies or obstacles here at all. Examine objects around the parlor and you're repeatedly told, "Nothing unusual."

Entering the parlor, though, I had to pass through a strangely tall room. The camera emphasized the verticality, peering at me like a child staring down at an ant through a magnifying glass.

I step back into that tall room with my new shotgun and the director takes control away just long enough to show me the ceiling pressing slowly downward. The room feels suddenly claustrophobic, and it's getting smaller. The door leading to the safety of the hallway is locked, so a player's only real option is retreat.

In Jill's case, though, the door back into the parlor is also locked. There's no way out. The ceiling grinds downward, slowly enough that you feel the anguish of anticipation, of futility, of regret. The game is making you pay for your greed, and it's making you watch.

And then, suddenly, we cut to Barry in the hallway, trying to get the door open.

He calls to you. Jill pleads to him for help.

The director is in control again. In Chris's route, this entire sequence is a puzzle to be solved. Here, though, it is revealed instead as a cinematic setpiece. Barry kicks down the door just in time. The two of you bond over some hideous dialogue.

> JILL: Oh, Barry!

> BARRY: That was too close. You were almost a JILL SANDWICH.

> JILL: Huh, you're right! Barry, thanks for saving my life.

> BARRY: *[stares blankly]*

Your bond with Barry grows stronger. This, in a house of monsters and death traps, is a friend. Maybe not the brightest friend, but a friend.

Oh, and, you get to keep the shotgun.

In Chris's route, this sequence goes quite differently.

Unlike Jill, Chris has nobody who will come to his rescue. Also unlike Jill, he can retreat: His parlor door doesn't lock. He can replace the shotgun. He can leave safely.

He can.

But that's not how things usually pan out for Chris.

In this route, the crushing ceiling isn't a trigger for an amusing cutscene; it's a monkey trap.

Though monkey traps have been used by actual hunters to catch actual prey, Robert M. Pirsig uses the concept to reflect on the human experience in his 1974 book, *Zen and the Art of Motorcycle Maintenance.* He describes a monkey trap as "a hollowed-out coconut chained to a stake. The coconut has some rice inside which can be grabbed through a small hole. The hole is big enough so that the monkey's hand can go in, but too small for his fist with rice in it to come out."

Other tellings refer to a box instead of a coconut, or to a banana instead of rice, but the central idea is the same. As Pirsig says of the monkey, "If he opens his hand he's free."[7]

---

7 For a more lighthearted illustration of the concept, refer to the *Simpsons* episode "Marge on the Lam," in which Homer can't remove his arm from a vending machine because he won't let go of a can of soda.

But that's not how things usually panned out for the monkey.

In the Spencer Mansion's monkey trap, the bait needs to be something players want so badly that they'll refuse to let go.

We're helpless in the Spencer Mansion. We're scrounging for ammo and ink ribbons. We're trying to progress and we're getting nowhere.

We need this shotgun. Teasing us with this new tool turns us into petulant Veruca Salts. We want it *now*.

The hunter approaches the monkey. The ceiling presses down.

The solution to Chris's puzzle—also an option for Jill—is to find a broken shotgun much later in the game and return to swap it for the functional one.

Eventually, you'll figure that out.

But not before you are ground into paste at least once, still clutching your banana.

ALL THE COLORS
OF THE DARK

WHENEVER I LOAD A SAVED FILE, *Resident Evil* welcomes me back with, "You have once again entered the world of survival horror."

Today the phrase "survival horror" is so familiar that it's easy to forget that it's *Resident Evil* that coined it. As Rod Serling did with *The Twilight Zone* and Joseph Heller did with *Catch-22*, *Resident Evil* took a concept we innately understood and gave it a name we wouldn't forget.

Genres allow us to curate works of art. When there's a particular emotion we'd like to feel—or, of course, avoid—genres are the signposts that tell us where to go.

They are also imperfect, however, which is why you'll see people debate whether *Pikmin* is a real-time strategy game or an adventure puzzler, whether *Hitman* is a stealth game or an action game, and whether *Metroid Prime* is a first-person shooter or a metroidvania. (When you're debating whether or not a game belongs in the genre named after its own series, you know things are getting hairy.) There was a high-profile example of genre confusion in 2018, when *Detroit: Become Human* won RPG of the Year at the Australian Game Awards, despite it having no recognizable RPG elements.

Survival horror, likewise, does not have a universally accepted definition. 1982's *Haunted House*, a game developed by Atari that I used to love without understanding how to play, is often cited as the earliest example of survival horror, but accepting it as one only makes it clear that we haven't established a firm definition.

Haunted House is horror-themed, at least. Your character is represented only by a set of eyeballs, the rest of you blending in with the pitch-black background. You can light a match to see the immediate area around you, and as you pop blindly from room to room you will find yourself pursued by bats, spiders, and ghosts, essentially the contents of the after-Halloween bargain bin at Party City.

Your goal is to find three pieces of a magic urn, which are randomly placed around the Graves Mansion. Sometimes you'll find them immediately, sometimes only after protracted exploration. There are things the game does fairly well. Your character's pupils point in the direction you're moving, which adds a hell of a lot of charm. And because the game couldn't handle convincing staircase animations, *Haunted House* approximates the concept by playing an ascending series of notes as you move to a higher floor, and a descending series of notes as you move to a lower one.

It's a notable early foray into creepy video games, but I think it's a massive stretch to classify it as survival horror.

A GameSpy article that classified it as one struggled to support its own argument. The author's survival horror checklist included such vague concepts as "creepy theme," "item collection," and "a variety of monsters." If you're subconsciously compiling a list of games that satisfy those conditions while also emphatically *not* being survival horror—*Ghosts 'n Goblins, Doom, The Witcher, Majora's Mask, Persona 3*—you'll understand the value of firmer definitions.

Establishing clear definitions helps to minimize confusion, which is an inherently good thing, but it can also lead to hair-splitting and gatekeeping.

Concerned by the increasing elasticity of the roguelike genre, attendees of the International Roguelike Development Conference in 2008 hosted a long discussion with the intention of developing a list of rules for roguelikes. That list is known as the Berlin Interpretation, which sounds like the first step toward punishing genre confusion as a war crime. It's an interesting read, if only to see how difficult it is to retroactively impose strict definition on an art form.

However well-intentioned, it received and continues to receive predictable pushback. Darren Grey, himself a roguelike developer, made his opinion known by titling his response "Screw the Berlin Interpretation!"

The elements outlined in the Berlin Interpretation range from the mechanical (random environment generation, permadeath) to matters of difficulty (complexity, tactical challenge) to the cosmetic (ASCII graphics, dungeons). By the end of their list, it's hard to say what the authors truly believe makes the roguelike unique, because their criteria cover so many different aspects of a game.

All of this is to say two things: If we're going to keep talking about survival horror, we need to define it; and, once we do, someone will write a blog post telling us to screw ourselves.

The very phrase "survival horror" brings with it both mechanical (survival) and emotional (horror) expectations, and it's worth thinking about how games can successfully meet both without leaning too far into either.

I don't want this to be my Berlin Interpretation, but I do want us to have some common language to build upon, with an open invitation to tweak, edit, refine, and outright fix.

In order of descending importance, here are what I believe are the nine defining elements of survival horror:

1. **Scarcity of resources.** Players shouldn't find healing items, crates of ammunition, or armor upgrades with anything like a reliable frequency, and there should be no way for first-time players to know when they will find more.

2. **Realistic protagonists.** Protagonists should have realistic physical and mental abilities. They should be relatively weak in both offense and defense. Hiding, sneaking, and otherwise avoiding combat should often be better options than fighting.

3. **Protagonists outside of their comfort zones.** Protagonists can hold any occupation, but they should not be operating within the realm of their normal experience. The protagonists' skills may help them succeed, but nothing about the game should be business as usual for them.

4. **Methodical progress.** Particular areas, sequences, and monsters can be designed in such a way to encourage rapid movement, but the game should unfold slowly overall. It should creep rather than barrel. Puzzles aid this, as reading clues and determining solutions slow the pace of progress.

5. **Severe penalty for failure.** Failure shouldn't feel like a temporary setback; it should feel catastrophic. There's little horror when facing a beast, no matter how hideous, if players know they can save their progress whenever they like.

6. **Fewer, stronger enemies.** Every enemy should pose an individual threat. Players shouldn't only have to learn to deal with enemies in general, but should have to learn to deal with every individual enemy in its own context. Enemies should also be deployed sparingly by developers to avoid making the game tedious.

7. **Active disempowerment.** Players should never feel well-equipped for long. The game may increase the protagonists' health, defense, or firepower, but this should be followed by more powerful enemies or other hazards, returning them to a state of vulnerability.

8. **Emphasis on atmosphere over story.** The game's story may be rich and rewarding, or it may feel like an afterthought. Either way, a frightening atmosphere is what is built, sustained, and explored throughout the game. Stories are often told through scattered logs, letters, and journal entries, preventing

the horror from being pushed aside for the sake of long, safe cutscenes.

9. **Lack of relief.** The player should never feel entirely at ease. Even in safe areas, they should wonder what they'll find next, or what will find them. Any respite they do find should be limited and temporary.

Defining doesn't have to mean restricting, or inspecting a game clinically to make sure it's checking all the boxes. It can mean a shared vocabulary. It can mean a better understanding of which aspects of a genre endure and remain effective. Perhaps most importantly, it can create a recognizable framework that playful artists can either lean into or subvert, modulating the experience based on audience expectations.

Resident Evil did not create most of survival horror's conventions, but it did solidify them. It became the template that subsequent games followed and built upon, and there's little that survival horror does today that isn't already present here, in the game that coined the phrase in the first place.

SHRIEK OF THE
MUTILATED

THE SHOTGUN TAKES ZOMBIES DOWN in just a few shots, and only one if you know the best way to use it: Aim diagonally upward, let the zombie get close enough, and then blast it right through the head. I'm rewarded for this knowledge with zombie heads popping like grapes and gore raining down around me.

It's fun, but I remember quickly enough that I now have another ammunition type to manage. I've hoarded more than 60 bullets for my default handgun, which is great, but if I want to use the shotgun I'm back to scrounging, and surely I should save the shells I do find for whatever stronger enemy I'm certain to encounter next.

I can either overpower my enemies right now, or I can keep them from overpowering me later. *Resident Evil*'s biggest gift to me so far is a gun I'd be stupid to use.

After a bit more exploration, I wind my way up to the second floor and end up back in the foyer. Barry is there, staring vacantly into the middle distance, which I'm pretty sure is the closest thing he has to a hobby.

We greet each other, and he says, "Whoa! This hall is dangerous!" despite the fact that this is one of the few safe areas in the entire game. He hands something to Jill.

JILL: What is it?

BARRY: It's a weapon! It's really powerful, especially against living things.

It's not a weapon; it's ammunition—acid rounds. And I doubt I need to spell out the problem with his "living things" line for you. I hope we eventually get a prequel in which we meet whatever mule kicked young Barry in the head.

I'll find the weapon that uses the acid rounds shortly, but I won't find it under pleasant circumstances.

In John Carpenter's 1982 film *The Thing*, American researchers in Antarctica explore a deserted Norwegian research station. Whatever happened left no survivors. There are documents. There is video. There are corpses. If the Americans are to avoid a similar fate, they will have to learn from the mistakes of those who already failed.

That's the advantage I have. I didn't go first.

In *Resident Evil*, the ill-fated Bravo team plays the role of our Norwegians. They go first. They do their best. And by the time we and the rest of Alpha team get there, they've already failed. If we can learn from their mistakes, if we can spot some detail they overlooked, we have a chance to end our story differently.

We already found the first Bravo, Kenneth, and seeing him get devoured meant we immediately knew that we're dealing with, at the very least, a violent and crazed cannibal. Kenneth may have thought the man was sick. He may have tried to help him. After all, wouldn't it be ridiculous to assume that the guy shuffling toward him was a zombie? Finding Kenneth's corpse gives us the in-game rationale to shoot the creature… something Kenneth did not have.

Leaving Barry, I head down a narrow corridor where blood is smeared on the wall and floor. I step out onto the veranda and find the next Bravo, vehicle specialist Forest Speyer, surrounded by crows that have been feasting on his innards.

Forest died clutching a bazooka, which is now ours for the taking. It was clearly not a lack of firepower that doomed him.

Before long we'll find communications expert Richard Aiken. Richard is alive, but he's been mortally wounded—a good clue to save the game before venturing further. Then we find mission leader Enrico Marini in the catacombs beneath the estate. In both a physical and an investigative sense, Enrico got closest to the truth, and he reveals that a member of STARS is a traitor before he's shot and killed from the shadows.

Each member of Bravo is a sign warning us of danger ahead, and the fact that they were our colleagues makes that danger feel genuine. These characters had the same training we had. If they died, it wasn't through ineptitude—it's because the Spencer Mansion is just that deadly.

Resident Evil positions us as the hero of one story and… well, we are. But before our arrival, a different story starring Bravo team began and ended.

An approach like this works well in horror because it relies on our imaginations. Piecing together the central mystery of the game, finding the slain members of Bravo, and poring over records left by the researchers who brought this nightmare to life is more satisfying and chilling than a cutscene showing us the same things could have ever been.

Resident Evil's backstory unfolds internally, in our minds.

The gradual piecing together of past tragedy is deeply appealing to me. I love connecting story elements for weeks or months in my mind after finishing a game. I don't just get to spend my time enjoying a story; I get to figure out for myself, piece by piece, what the story *is*.

This is part of the reason Fallout is one of my favorite series. The games vary in quality, but there's one consistent highlight: the Vaults.

The Vaults are underground shelters that allowed humanity to survive a devastating nuclear war. Like *Resident Evil*'s Umbrella, though, the Vault-Tec Corporation had its own agenda: As long as human beings are sealed up together, why not experiment on them a bit?

Exploring a Vault is such an intriguing experience because, in almost every case, we discover it long after its occupants have perished. Vault-Tec's cruel experiments echo symbolically through the empty corridors. We use terminal entries, audio logs, corpses, and environmental details to piece together in our minds what happened— the events of the *Twilight Zone* episode we just missed.

Many of *Resident Evil*'s biggest moments came and went before we picked up the controller. A cascade of tragedy consumed the House of Spencer, and our Bravo colleagues made fatal mistakes so that we wouldn't have to.

There's no opportunity to mourn Forest. As soon as we take the bazooka, we're swarmed by still-hungry crows. It's just as well: My inventory is full, and I need to find a storage box.

Barry is gone when I return to the main hall, and I'm about to spend a long stretch of the game alone.

If I were playing as Chris, though, I'd be just about to find some companionship.

IN THE MOUTH
OF MADNESS

THE SECOND SAVE ROOM is in the Spencer Mansion's west wing, and there's nothing of interest here for Jill. There is a shelf full of chemicals and a bed against the wall, but the only relevant items are the storage box and the typewriter.

That's probably why, during my Chris run, I jumped in surprise when I opened the door and got a face full of some kind of gas.

As Chris, this is where you'll meet Rebecca, the lone survivor of Bravo team and his companion character. She was hiding in here to keep safe, and you can't really blame her for macing you the moment you appear.

CHRIS: Whaaat?! What is it!?

REBECCA: Ohhh! Ohhhhhhhh noooooooooh!

The fact that most players share a collective chuckle over Barry and have completely forgotten Rebecca is proof enough in itself that we nearly always play the game as Jill. It's worth a run-through as Chris just to experience a whole other helping of *Resident Evil*'s voice acting.

Rebecca's voice seems to alternate between that of a 30-something woman and a three-year-old girl, from calm to manic, from capable to incompetent in the space between two sentences.

I got a great laugh out of a number of unexpected exchanges. For example, Rebecca asked if she could come with me. I accepted.

> CHRIS: Alright, let's do it.
>
> REBECCA: Yes, sir! I'll do my best.
>
> CHRIS: *[pregnant pause]*
>
> REBECCA: I have to prepare something. Would you like to go ahead?

I chose to bring her with me, she acknowledged this, and then she made an excuse to stay behind. It's *Resident Evil* realizing it hasn't quite thought this part through, then saying, "Actually, forget I brought it up." It's fantastic.

Resident Evil's voice acting is the stuff of legend. We can close our eyes and hear the strange delivery of Wesker's "Stop it. Don't o-pen *that DOOR!*"

Or Richard's, "There are terrible demons. Ouuuuhhch."

Or Rebecca's, "Look at those *monstoooooors!*"

Or Chris's, "You call this FAILure, your SAVior?"

Or Barry's, "But just TAKE-a-LOOK-at-THIS!"

Or Barry's, "Wesker is a crazyman!"

Or Barry's, "I'll just go and get some fresh air and be EATEN BY A MONSTER."

Or pretty much anything that Barry says.

And those are just the bizarre readings. There's another layer of comedy when the lines don't fit the context, such as the scene in which Jill asks, "Will you wait here?" to Chris, who is locked in a jail cell.

Or when Jill calmly explains, "It can't control what it does," to a coldcocked Barry.

Or when Barry asks, "Have you found anything interesting?" immediately after walking through the smoldering remains of a giant serpent.

Or when Barry…

…man. Poor Barry.

The voice acting is one of *Resident Evil*'s most significant and infamous charms, and I couldn't resist learning as much as I could about the game's voice actors.

As with the live-action stars of the game, a number of the voice actors have yet to be identified. What's more, they aren't credited in the game at all, fueling a widespread misconception that the live actors and voice actors were the same.

Well, okay, there's one voice actor who receives credit: Ward Sexton.

Sexton's is the voice that snarls the title at you whenever you have the temerity to boot up *Resident Evil*.

The odds are good you've heard Sexton in many different contexts. He's narrated trailers and commercials for *Modern Family*, *Iron Chef America*, *Tangled*, American Express, Apple, Kellogg's, and much more.

I assumed Sexton was cast in *Resident Evil* through the Inagawa Motoko Office, but I was wrong; Sexton was a lone wolf. "I never worked for IMO," he told me. "IMO is someone who always chased me around. It sounds really terrible, but I didn't need representation in Japan."

Long before *Resident Evil* started development, Sexton had built up a personal brand as one of the best voiceover artists in the industry. He was known—and is still known to many—as "The VO." The fact that he is the only voice actor to receive credit in the game is evidence of his clout.

"My life from 1985 until I left Japan in 2011 was pretty much in the studio," he said. "I did probably over 1,000 jobs a year."

Sexton grew up in Hawaii and moved to Tokyo in 1981, where his career took off.

"It was just accidental," he told me. "The timing and everything else was really right. At that time there was a lot of voiceover work to be done." There were also relatively few English-language voiceover artists in the Tokyo area. "The guys who were there weren't very good. I was one of the few people who showed up there as a professional. I had worked in advertising and I had developed the reputation."

That reputation as something of a voiceover rock star is not something he cultivated deliberately.

"I kind of turned the industry on its ear," he said. "One guy said that even though he could afford an expensive car, he would never dare drive his expensive car to the studio because the producers or directors would not like that. That's very Japan. And I didn't know anything about that."

Sexton drove his Porsche to gigs, which gave him a striking and recognizable identity among the rest of the talent pool. "I would drive it, and everyone would go, 'Oh, it's the Porsche guy!' It worked to my advantage. It was a marketing tool for me, almost, annoyingly." He laughed. "I just wanted to be proud of my car!"

Another way he bucked the trend was by not signing with a management company. He also didn't sign with any agents because, he explained, "what they call agents there are actually management companies." Any clients who wanted his services had to set their terms directly with him.

"There were very few what you'd call 'professional voiceovers,'" Sexton told me. "Barry's one. Lynn, too. Scott McCulloch."

Those were people he knew well, who would eventually go on to voice characters in *Resident Evil*. Barry Gjerde voiced Barry, Lynn Harris voiced Rebecca, and Scott McCulloch voiced Chris.

Gjerde was born Oddbjørn Egil Gjerde. He adopted the name Barry as a young boy when his family moved from Norway to Canada, as it was easier for his new friends to pronounce. He told me that he can trace his interest in voice acting and narrating to the shows he watched as a child.

"I remember watching Disney documentaries on TV," he said. "There was one about animals and their journey. I remember the sound of the narrator's voice. He had a good delivery and his humor put a smile on my face. I didn't—and still don't—know who he was, and I didn't then know the word 'narrator.'"

Living in Norway and Canada and watching television from America and England meant he was exposed to a number of different accents in his formative years, and he became fascinated with speech. Around 1959, at age seven or eight, he started paying attention to voices in his favorite shows, from *The Flintstones* to the 1950s British series *The Adventures of Robin Hood*.

"It was the Robin Hood show that made me wonder why some people pronounced the word no as *nøu*," he said via email, "while others pronounced it the way I did, in my regular Canadian English. Sometimes, it was just a phrase I heard. I remember mimicking 'Verrry interesting…' in a German accent like Arte Johnson on the hilarious and very groundbreaking 1960s comedy show, *Rowan & Martin's Laugh-In*. And I would make up my own voices. I just liked to do that."

He'd also find himself making faces in the mirror to impersonate comedians he'd seen on *The Ed Sullivan Show*. The performance bug had officially bitten him, and by 1969 he was reading the news for the radio station at the University of British Columbia.

Gjerde moved to Tokyo in 1982, where his skill with language brought him work as an English teacher and translator. A few years later, he was able to start a career in performing.

"It wasn't voice acting to begin with," he told me. "It was narration for industry, culture, business, English education materials, banking… very corporate. I approached some agencies and we hit it off. Narration was a good step up from teaching English. As my narration voice became known in Tokyo, the scope of my work expanded to include character voices."

Gjerde crossed paths with Sexton a number of times, and the two became friends. In 1992, Sexton hired him for a major project: an English dub of Studio Ghibli's *Porco Rosso*.

"Japan Airlines wanted an English dub of *Porco Rosso* they could show on their flights," Sexton said. While it was flattering that they wanted him to manage the project, he doubted that he could find a voice cast that could do justice to the material. "I knew Studio Ghibli really well. I said, 'You guys have got to get this done in Los Angeles. This is just too big a thing to do here.' And they said, 'No, Japan Airlines wants it on their flight.'"

Sexton acquiesced, against his better judgment.

Gjerde recorded his lines on June 8 in a session that lasted around two or three hours.

"While the movie is called *Porco Rosso* these days, at the time of the Japan Airlines recording, we knew it as *The Crimson Pig*, an obvious translation from the Italian," he said.

Gjerde played a number of characters, most notably the weaponsmith. He also voiced a radio presenter, an announcer, and the man speaking to Porco on the telephone early in the film.

"Let me set the record straight," Gjerde told me. "I did *not* play the lead role. Recently, I have read comments online stating that I was the lead voice actor. Not so. The lead role was played by Ward Sexton."

This is indeed in conflict with a large number of sources that credit Gjerde as Porco, but having tracked down the Japan Airlines dub on an out-of-print Region 2 Japanese release, I established that it's clearly Sexton's voice, and both actors confirmed this to me. Sexton further told me that Lynn Harris voiced deuteragonist Fio and a number of the film's children.

Sexton's concerns about the quality of the dub have proven to be well-founded; it's since been entirely overshadowed by Disney's high-budget 2004 English dub starring Michael Keaton.

Three years later, Sexton found himself raising similar doubts about another project he was working on with Gjerde and Harris: *Resident Evil*.

Again, Sexton suggested recording with voice talent in Los Angeles, as well as getting better writers. "With the *Resident Evil* stuff, I thought, 'You've got to get this rewritten. Even if these guys do read it pretty well, it doesn't sound very natural,' you know?" he said. "It was difficult."

Poor writing was one of Sexton's biggest pet peeves during his time in Japan.

"In a five-year period, I literally slept an average of three hours per night," he told me. "That's because I would constantly, whether they liked it or not, rewrite all these scripts. I would come home from the studio and then sit in front of my computer and start rewriting. I would be in the studio from 10:00 until 10:00, or 12:00 to 12:00, then come home and rewrite scripts. Then, hopefully, catch a couple hours' sleep before I had to be at the studio again."

Sexton made his own job harder on himself, but that reinforced his reputation as a high-quality voiceover artist.

"A lot of guys would just go in there and they'd end up with a crappy English script that some Japanese person wrote that makes absolutely no sense," he said. "And they'd think, 'I'm not paid to do the scripts, so therefore I will read this crappy English script and forget it.' I refused to do that. With my work ethic, I certainly couldn't do that. Because I'm half-Japanese, I didn't want them to be embarrassed overseas. Plus, I didn't want my voice on something that sounded funky."

Once again, his concerns were dismissed, and the infamous script and performances of *Resident Evil* were born.

"For those that do not know, a recording session is not a democracy," Gjerde told Monique Alves of Resident Evil Database. "It is the performance of a script that is created after long preparation and decision-making by people that the voice actors have usually never met. The voice actor is there to deliver lines written by someone else, and under the guidance of the director, who works to satisfy the client's vision."

A voice actor may be given bad lines, but it is still his job to deliver those lines. In addition, *Resident Evil* featured many first-time voice actors, and Gjerde told Alves that the physical conditions of the recording booth made for uncomfortable sessions. It was around five feet wide and six feet long, and at times four voice actors were crammed inside, reaching over each other and ducking out of the way so they could all use a single microphone.

According to Gjerde's records, he recorded his lines in two sessions in 1995: one on August 12 and the next on September 5. He remembers being shown Barry's cutscenes as he was recording the lines.

"I used my own natural voice to start, not my corporate narration voice, and since I received no instruction to do otherwise, I continued with that," Gjerde told me. "In retrospect, and as I was getting into the storyline while recording, I wish I had used a voice that was gruffer and tougher, something with more of an edge to it. I did get asked to do certain lines over again. That is very normal in the course of a recording session. But, again, I received no instruction to change my voice or tone."

Barry Burton became a fan favorite, but not in a way that pleases Gjerde.

"I feel that not enough attention was given to shaping the characters, sitting down with the voice actors and explaining what they wanted," he said. "Having many voice actors in the studio at the same time, some recording and some waiting to record, meant that there was little chance for a one-to-one discussion with the people in charge or the director. That would mean more time to record everyone, which would mean more money for studio time."

If it sounds like Gjerde is shifting the blame for his own shortcomings, it shouldn't take more than a cursory listen to his wider body of work to convince you otherwise. He's narrated material for Sony, Toyota, Budweiser, and even voiced the beloved Pepsiman in a number of advertisements. Perhaps the strongest proof that Barry Burton is not a fair example of Gjerde's talents is the work he's done for Classic Gallery, a classical music program for passengers aboard All Nippon Airways. Gjerde introduces the experience, and his relaxed, professional, soothing tone is light-years away from the strangled performance we hear in *Resident Evil*.

Gjerde shared Sexton's concerns about the writing.

"I personally dislike the poor lines my character was given," he told me. "The weakness of the script demonstrates the importance of preparing English, or any other target language, at a native-speaker level. It made me feel that, when you get down to it, good writers are more important than actors."

Sexton's voice is only heard in the game reciting the title and the names of the major characters, but he recorded much more during his session.

"I showed up to do it and they said, 'Well, we'll pay you now, but can you do Biohazard zero through ten?'" Sexton laughed. "And so I did Biohazard zero through ten and Resident Evil zero through ten, all in one session."

As a result, his distinctive growl welcomes players to the Eastern and Western versions of subsequent games, even though Capcom never called him back into the studio.

"I almost blew out my pipes!" he said. "I couldn't work the rest of that day, almost. It was awful."

The session took such a toll on him because he was directed to shout the title rather than speak it, a decision he did not feel was wise.

"I told them at the beginning, 'You don't do this. You don't scream at a mic.' Instead you get up on the mic and you go [*firmly*] 'Biohazard,' or something like that, but they didn't get it. They made me scream in a scary voice! Instead of 'Biohazard Zero, Biohazard One,' it would be 'BIOHAZARD ZERO. BIOHAZARD ONE.' I hate listening to it now."

The high volume of his performance also made the Western title far more difficult to pull off than the original title.

"The way they wanted me to read it, 'Biohazard' was a lot easier than 'Resident Evil,'" he explained. "Resident Evil, because it starts with an R, it's hard to get a grip on that sound. You know? It's just harder to do. If they allowed me to do it the way we do it here in the States, it wouldn't have been so hard. It would have saved my voice, and it would have been a lot better."

Sexton told me he actually prefers the work of the other announcers used in the spinoffs to his own performance.

Scott McCulloch, from Victoria, British Columbia, ended up voicing Chris. He also played Richter Belmont in 1997's *Castlevania: Symphony of the Night*, giving him the distinction of voicing main characters in two of the PlayStation's defining titles, as well as two of the most influential games in history. Outside of voice acting, he was a popular DJ on Tokyo's InterFM.

"I first met Scott in Tokyo," Gjerde told me. "We would run into each other from time to time, sometimes at train stations, sometimes at studios, and we would talk. He was a very easygoing fellow. I remember hearing him on the radio and thinking that he truly did have a good DJ voice."

McCulloch bonded with Gjerde as a fellow Canadian. He also became good friends with Sexton.

"He was a handsome dude," Sexton said. "He even modeled, and he had a lot of women chasing after him, and the whole bit."

By the time of *Resident Evil*, however, things had changed.

"He got a little overweight and he wasn't looking very healthy," Sexton said. "In the end he smoked pretty heavily. I was really surprised to find out later on that he had passed."

McCulloch died in September of 2000, his career cut short after only five years in the industry. Gjerde and Sexton were both hit hard by his death.

"He was younger than I was," Sexton said. "That kind of… really kind of got to me."

"I went to his funeral wake and I saw Scott lying there before me in an open casket," Gjerde told Alves. "I also met his widow and their young daughter. This had a great impact on me. […] Never had I seen a friend deceased in a coffin. Scott's funeral wake was on Friday, September 29, 2000. I will never forget it. Many members of Tokyo's foreign voice talent community came to pay their respects."

Another example of misinformation being spread on the internet is McCulloch's cause of death, which many sources list, without citation, as a traffic accident. Neither Sexton nor Gjerde agree with this.

"It is my understanding that he had a brain aneurysm that ruptured," Gjerde told me. "He spent about two weeks in hospital, and then had a second aneurysmal episode that, very sadly, took his life."

Just as with her live-action counterpart, fans have yet to identify the actor who voiced Jill.

"I remember the actress playing Jill was from northern Alberta, Canada," Gjerde told Alves. "She was asking another Canadian actor if he had attended NAIT, the Northern Alberta Institute of Technology, which is in Edmonton and where she had studied. It was not her first time voice acting."

There has also been no positive identification of the actor who voiced Wesker. Gjerde does remember Dean Harrington—the announcer from *Super Smash Bros. Melee*, among other things—doing a voice, and IMDb credits him as voicing Enrico Marini. Harrington himself, however, has dismissed this, telling Project Umbrella that he did record lines but doesn't recognize his voice in the game and can't be sure that his role wasn't cut.

This meant that I'd managed to get in touch with every known surviving actor—voice or live-action—aside from Lynn Harris. In addition to playing Rebecca, both Harrington and Gjerde confirmed she directed the game's voice actors, albeit without credit. I reached out through colleagues, friends, and family. Eventually a voice actor who knows Harris politely informed me that she prefers to avoid media contact.

Sexton considers Harris a friend, though at the time of our conversation he hadn't spoken to her in a while. "Lynn does a lot of children's voices," he said. "She's a tall woman, but she can sound like a five-year-old pretty easily."

Gjerde told me that he remembers her working to get many members of Tokyo's voiceover community listed on IMDb along with their projects, as they weren't receiving credit for their work. I admire her dedication to resolving incomplete and inaccurate information all the more after sifting through so many false leads for this book.

In the aftermath of the game's release, Gjerde—suddenly known for delivering the worst lines in a game full of worst lines—was understandably frustrated, and he took the criticism to heart.

"There was a surprising amount of verbal abuse on web forums about *Resident Evil*," he told me. "It was vilifying and vituperative. Taking down my webpage and avoiding game-related sites distanced me from those who hid behind their keyboards making verbal attacks."

Gjerde deleted his personal website—and its invitation to contact him—around 2005.

"I built the site to see if I could do it, and I succeeded," he said. "I did advertise my work and gave links to interesting sites, but the fun had kind of gone out of it."

Eventually, though, he started to take the criticism in stride.

"It did hurt at first, but you can't be too thin-skinned if you're a performer," he said. "After a while, I told myself to not take it all too seriously. I think that a lot of the negative feedback was from a small minority of players. Some negative feedback is a part of life, and you just have to get used to it. Conversely, I had positive feedback from people for whom the game was part of their childhood years."

Both Gjerde and Sexton remain active in the voice-over industry, with the latter having a significant presence in horror trailers.

"I did the movie trailers for *Resident Evil* in Japan," he said. "Or obviously *Biohazard* over there. You see the trailer and you hear, 'Milla Jovovich, *Biohazard*.' That's me. I did *Silent Hill* as well. *Sinister, Insidious, The Ring,* and stuff like that. I'm not a big fan of horror, by the way, but I've got the voice for it, apparently."

He really does. It's almost strange to hear Sexton introducing anything other than horror. He can sell a sunny day as well as he can sell a dark and stormy night, but the latter definitely comes naturally to him. Perhaps a bit too naturally.

"I have actually had [VO] directors [of horror trailers] come down and say I sound too scary. And I was like… what?" He laughed. "And so I got this reputation for being that horror guy. When I did the trailer for *The Grudge*, called *Ju-on* in Japan, they literally toned it down so much because there were complaints that kids could not sleep when they saw that trailer on TV."

Gjerde is also not a horror fan. "I don't mind spooky and creepy," he said, but, "they don't necessarily add up to horror." He does enjoy *The Twilight Zone*, however, and he told me he gets a kick out of Don Knotts in *The Ghost and Mr. Chicken*.

Though Sexton looks back on his career with fondness, his memories are not all positive. He told me about one arcade game for which he provided a voice. "All of a sudden they were using my voice in the commercials and all kinds of different places," he said. He reached out to the company to let them know that hadn't been part of the agreement. "They said, 'Go ahead and sue us. Do what you want. We'll make sure you never work in Japan again.'"

Ultimately, his reputation ended up working against him.

"Being known as The VO was flattering at first, but it became a huge burden later," he said. "After the voiceover bubble burst, my status just meant I was expensive."

Sexton is 66 as of this writing. He lives in Arizona with his wife and family, but one of his jobs in Tokyo continues to this day. "I am still the voice of *Music Station*," he said, "the longest-running live TV music broadcast in Japan."

Music Station, which debuted in 1986, is similar in format to MTV's *Total Request Live* or the BBC's *Top of the Pops*. Sexton says he and host Kazuyoshi Morita—going by the professional name Tamori—are the only two original talents left on the program, but technically Hiroshi Sekiguchi preceded Tamori as host for less than one year.[8]

---

8 In 1986, Tamori left his own small stamp on another legendary series; his likeness replaced the piranha plant in an official, modified version of *Super Mario Bros.* released to promote the Japanese radio show *All Night Nippon*.

Sexton's marathon day of recording means he'll stay part of the franchise until Capcom decides not to use his voice anymore, and his reading of those words is so iconic that it's difficult to even see the phrase "Resident Evil" without hearing it in his voice.[9]

"I'm grateful and all that," Sexton said, "but I don't get money forever for that. It was just one payment. Had I gotten any kind of residuals I'd be sitting a lot prettier."

Sexton realizes how fortunate he was to stumble into such a long career.

"I was just lucky," he said. "The timing and everything worked out. I got on a roll real fast, I had a good reputation, and I became a big shot over there. I'm... not one here." He laughed. "Well, I guess I kind of am. I just got this call saying, 'We want to use your voice, could you do this? We can't pay as much, but here's what we can offer.' And it's still pretty decent."

Hopefully, though, one day Capcom will invite him back to record titles for Resident Evil 11 through 20.

---

9 We may sadly be at that point, as *Resident Evil 7* does not have its title narrated.

I EAT YOUR SKIN

I STEER JILL DEEPER INTO the west wing and find a door that she masterfully unlocks. It's a bedroom, and we find some evidence of human activity. There's an unmade bed, clutter on the floor, a journal on a desk. It's been easy to assume that *somebody* lived in the Spencer Mansion at some point, but this room proves it.

I approach the desk, where a small lamp quite literally spotlights the journal. Our invisible director is working hard to prevent us from missing what we're meant to see.

One of my biggest surprises on this playthrough is how few logs and journals there actually are. In the version of *Resident Evil* that lives in my memory, they were everywhere. Perhaps I remembered them being more plentiful than they were because reading them was my favorite part of the experience.

Resident Evil succeeded at making me feel afraid, making me panic, and cultivating in me a sense of constant vulnerability. Those were things it wanted to do, and it had its fun doing them. The logs, however? Those were *my* fun.

Resident Evil tapped—for its own purposes—into my love of reading. It was great finding a green herb tucked away in the shadows, but it felt so much better to find a new book or letter or document to read. I was impressed and flattered by the game's assurance that even here, now, with the undead stalking the hallways and the unknowable stretches of Hell open before us, reading could still do us some good.

Strictly speaking, nearly all of the logs are optional pickups. If you skip them, miss them, or don't care to pay attention to them, though, significant swaths of story will pass you by. For you, that may be okay. For me? Not a chance.

Resident Evil was far from the first game to incorporate findable reading materials, but it was the first game I played in which these reading materials felt organic to the situation. A developer wasn't just squirreling away clues in some optional text boxes… these were pages scrawled by the hopeless, the desperate, the dying. These were windows into a lost history. These were crucial pieces of a puzzle that could fit together and reveal the secrets of the Spencer Mansion.

I reach for the book—probably the most effective bait to catch me in a monkey trap—and a zombie bursts out of the closet. It's a neat trick; the way the scene is blocked, you're guaranteed to have your back to the zombie as it appears, making for a perfectly composed "It's behind you!" moment.

No big deal, though. By now I've faced enough of these things. The zombie may have the element of surprise and some very cramped quarters on its side, but I take it down quickly enough.

At least, I think I do. I neglected to look for the pool of blood that signifies the true death of a zombie, and he grabs my leg as I step over him. It's surprising enough that, in real life, I jump. He bites into Jill's ankle and, without any input from me, she kicks his head clean off his body. It bounces around the room like a soccer ball. The scary movie briefly became a horror comedy.

With the pest out of the way, I actually read the journal, referred to in-game as the Keeper's Diary.

This is the precise moment *Resident Evil* first clicked for me, all those years ago. Until I found this, I assumed we were operating within a standard "escape the haunted house before it kills you" framework, much as I'd already experienced in *AitD* or… um… *Haunted House*.

The Keeper's Diary told me I was wrong. I was just one character in a much larger story.

The diary begins May 9, 1998, around two months before the events of the game. The keeper recounts a poker game with a guard named Scott, a researcher named

Steve, and somebody named Alias.[10] He refers to Steve as a "scumbag" and accuses him of cheating.

These are coworkers, but with titles like researcher, guard, and keeper (as opposed to, say, secretary, accountant, and junior records management specialist), there's clearly something more going on than four colleagues whiling away the hours between shifts.

In the May 10 entry, that something is revealed. The keeper describes being assigned to "a new monster," which looks "like a gorilla without any skin." He's instructed to feed it live food, so he tosses it a pig. He watches the monster play with, torture, and disembowel it.

Then, on May 11, tragedy. Scott storms into the keeper's room at around 5 a.m. The keeper reveals his distance from the actual research and experiments being conducted by not recognizing the hazmat suit Scott is wearing. Scott instructs the keeper to put one on. There has been an accident.

Whoever is in charge of this mysterious project implements quarantine. Nobody is allowed to leave or contact the outside world. A researcher—insane, infected, frustrated, or some combination of the three—calls the guards' bluff and attempts to leave the Spencer Mansion. He's shot dead.

---

10 Possibly a mistranslation of "Elias," but every port and the game's fully rewritten remake retain "Alias."

The keeper's subsequent entries complain of his skin smelling "musty." He develops a swelling on his back and his feet blister so badly he can barely walk. Five days after the accident, he reports that his entire body burns and itches. He scratches his arm and necrotic flesh sloughs away.

It's easy to connect these descriptions to the creatures we've seen shambling around the Spencer Mansion. We've seen the rotting flesh. We've seen the pained shuffling. We figured that these things used to be humans, but what this diary reveals is that they used to be *people*.

The keeper writes of an increase in feelings of cruelty and aggression. At one point he chooses to not feed the dogs… a preview of monstrous behavior to come. And then, by the May 19 entry, the keeper as he once knew himself is gone. He murders Scott because of his "ugly face" and eats him. The final entry, dated "4," reads only "Itchy. Tasty."[11]

So much story, so much revelation, told surprisingly well in the span of ten brief entries. Offhand references to a basement lab, a company, and a high-ranking researcher thrust me immediately from one kind of

_____

11 "4" may not mean June 4. In Japan, 4 is considered an unlucky number, similar to the way Westerners view 13. The reason for this is that 4's pronunciation, "shi," is the same as the Japanese word for death.

game into another. Monsters aren't roaming the halls because we're playing a horror game; monsters are roaming the halls because *somebody put them there*.

The Keeper's Diary is strongly reminiscent of 1835's "Diary of a Madman," a work of literary horror by Nikolai Gogol, presented as a journal by a man going gradually insane. It begins with relatively benign descriptions of the man's work, frustrations, and ambitions, but the entries soon become stranger and less grounded in what we recognize as reality. He writes of talking dogs, and of the letters they compose. ("The handwriting is somewhat doggish," he tells us.) He complains of feelings of weakness and fatigue as his madness consumes him.

Toward the end, he loses his grasp of time. He leaps forward to "The year 2000: April 43rd." Later entries are dated "February 30," "Marchember 86," and "January in the same year, following after February." My personal favorite is "No date. The day had no date."

Today it's not difficult to find literary influence in gaming, whether it's thematic, like the elaborate critique of Randian objectivism in 2007's *BioShock*, or direct, like the homage to Ray Bradbury's "There Will Come Soft Rains" in 2008's *Fallout 3*, with its house of mechanical convenience going mindlessly about its duties long after the occupants were killed in a nuclear apocalypse.

Resident Evil was the first game I knew that had a literary approach to storytelling. Yes, *AitD* was inspired by—and makes frequent reference to—Lovecraft, but the Hartwood Mansion really *is* just some haunted house. Its revelations aren't layered; there are monsters roaming around, and some text tells you how to kill them. *Resident Evil* goes deeper, hiding a more disturbing narrative beneath its floorboards.

Some of the logs don't just sketch in the backstory, but gradually reveal what's happening here, right now, to me. For instance, in a much later room, I find a security memo dated July 22, 1998, two days before the start of the game. "Lure the members of STARS into the lab and have them fight with the BOW in order to obtain data of actual battles," is the first instruction printed here. The last is to destroy the lab, "including all researchers and lab animals in a manner which will seem accidental."

It's from the pharmaceutical company Umbrella, headquartered in Raccoon City.

The things we've already read about viruses and experiments and labs suddenly have a lot more context. Rebecca helps Chris piece things together a little more clearly—he never was much one for thinkin' and connectin'—but this alone proves that the still-unfolding disaster is a step in somebody's plan. Bravo was lured here and knowingly slaughtered. Now we're here and not doing much better. STARS isn't just being eliminated; it is being eliminated as a test of Umbrella's bioorganic weapons.

This is a massive reveal, and perhaps the game's most important one. We're guinea pigs, and we learn this just as the danger from the BOWs ratchets up. "We have enough data on the zombies," I can imagine some Umbrella researcher saying in a *Cabin in the Woods*-style control room. "Let's unleash the next monster and see how she copes."

Reveals like this occur throughout *Resident Evil*'s logs. Sometimes small (a whistleblower, now infected, pleads to his dearest Ada[12] to go public with what happened), sometimes large (the name "A. Wesker" buried in the text of some security procedures), but always important to the unravelling of the conspiracy. What elevated *Resident Evil* above other games that asked me to kill some monsters was how expertly this game gradually unmasked the monster behind the monsters.

Resident Evil's texts are brief, consisting of a few paragraphs at most. These notes, diaries, and clippings gradually assemble a horrifying chronology, a storytelling mechanism that can be traced at least as far back

---

12 Sexy acrobat karate enthusiast Ada Wong, *Resident Evil*'s resident Mata Hari, who we won't meet until the sequel.

as Bram Stoker's 1897 novel, *Dracula*. *Dracula* is an epistolary novel, meaning it functions structurally as a sort of fictional scrapbook. Journals, letters, articles, and other sources comprise the entirety of the text. It's the literary origin of what film would eventually call found-footage horror. Movies have made it easy to forget that Dracula himself rarely appears in the novel, as most of the sources in Stoker's scrapbook are narrated from a necessary distance. As in *Resident Evil*, the actual story unfolds in its own background. Only when the scattered evidence is collected can we piece together what happened.

Alone in the Dark similarly used logs to convey its hints and backstory, but they're long, dense tomes without any clear indication of what's important and what's window dressing. It's fair to say that *AitD*'s logs are better written than the clunky, strained translations we find in *Resident Evil*, but *AitD* isn't a collection of short stories; it's a video game, and the meandering texts hinder the experience.

Frédéric Raynal discussed *AitD*'s logs at the 2012 Game Developers Conference. "If you read all the books, you have all the clues to kill the monsters," he explained. "I really wanted to force the player to find other solutions [besides] brutal force."

This is a great impulse that led to one of the defining features of survival horror, but ultimately Raynal defeated his own purpose. Because his logs were so lengthy and unfocused, it was difficult for players to realize they were reading clues, and many of those clues were not actionable. One long book, for instance, explains which of the game's many weapons will kill the vagabond, but there's no in-game way to identify the vagabond as the whirl of disconnected purple cubes in the library. Players still had to resort to brute force.

Resident Evil's logs are integrated better into the gameplay experience. They're short enough that they don't interrupt the pace of the game, and their relevance is clear enough that we don't stop midway through a document to wonder why we're bothering to read it.

The logs scattered around the Spencer Mansion are the only reason we're able to piece the real story back together. And each time we save our game at a typewriter, we're typing up our own experiences, writing our own logs, perhaps to be found by some later traveler if we don't succeed, perhaps to help him accomplish what we did not.

THE TWO FACES OF FEAR

THERE ARE CERTAIN THINGS I understand about the ways in which *Resident Evil* builds its atmosphere, modulates its pacing, and structures its scares. These are the things I can process and appreciate with a critical eye.

For example, there's Yawn, the gigantic snake that serves as the game's first boss. Facing him when I was younger resulted in a terrified panic, and I'm sure that's exactly the response *Resident Evil* wanted me to have. Now, I can step back a bit and enjoy the way the game achieves that response.

Just a couple of doors before we meet Yawn, I find Richard, dying painfully. He tells me he was bitten by a huge, poisonous snake.

> RICHARD: There is serum. Oh, no. I
> should have brought some with me.

It might seem pretty dumb for Richard to find serum in a house full of monsters and *not* take it with him, but his idiocy is plot-dictated: Jill and Chris can't take the serum if they find it earlier, either.

Whether we sprint to retrieve the serum or dawdle, he dies. Richard's death—and the specificity of his warning—should make it clear that serious danger is ahead. But just in case it doesn't, *Resident Evil* demonstrates some suspicious generosity by leaving two green herbs, two kinds of ammo (including one that's really powerful, especially against living things), and some ink ribbons. There are also bloody handprints on the wall. The only thing missing is a sign that says, "Save now, you big dummy."

With the tension appropriately ramped up, *Resident Evil* is ready to introduce us to Yawn, but first it toys with us just a little more. We need to advance far into Yawn's room before he pops up. We know something is coming, but we know neither what nor when. By the time it appears, we're far from the only exit and in immediate danger.

As soon as we see Yawn, our instinct is to flee. His head alone is about the size of Jill, and he can indeed swallow her whole. He absorbs a huge amount of ammunition from anything other than the bazooka, and the rounds for that weapon are rare. He deals massive damage and takes little in return.

Running in an attempt to avoid his attacks is the only viable—and rational—strategy, but it causes the camera to shift frequently between different angles, each time cutting him out of view. We lose track of exactly where he is, and when his drooling head bobs once more into frame, we have no choice but to keep moving, causing the camera to shift again. The cycle repeats. All *Resident Evil*'s invisible director has to do is convince us to keep moving, and we end up editing our own terrifying sequence. In horror, the more you see of a creature, the less scary it gets. Long, unbroken shots of a monster allow us to become familiar with it, to acclimatize to it, to notice the zippers and strings and CGI that create the illusion.

Stephen Spielberg famously—and inadvertently—learned this lesson while making 1975's *Jaws*. There were so many problems with the mechanical shark that he could not film his monster as he intended. He wondered, "What would Hitchcock do in a situation like this?" Hitchcock's hypothetical answer, illustrated by the darting knife in *Psycho*, was to show very little. Unquestionably, *Jaws* benefitted. Instead of being able to show us something scary, Spielberg was forced to *convince* us something was scary.

Resident Evil, consciously or not, faced the same problem. The longer we look at Yawn, the more opportunity we have to see the simplicity of his polygons, become familiar with his animations, realize he's just following an algorithm and therefore—fatally for the genre—nothing to be afraid of.

The spoken and silent warnings ahead of time, the cramped room, even the clunky and stuffy controls: Every piece works in harmony to create a boss fight that doubles as a fantastic horror setpiece.

But that's just what is happening on the screen, within the game. What I can't talk about with any authority is the other half of the fear equation: What's going on inside of me?

Enter Margee Kerr, a sociologist who studies fear and author of the book *Scream: Chilling Adventures in the Science of Fear*.

She told me that fear is an especially interesting subject to her because researchers have spent a lot of time approaching it the wrong way.

"I think we're kind of going into a new era of understanding emotions," she said. "Most of the research that happened during the 20th century has approached emotions as these discrete things. This is anger, this is fear, this is happiness, this is sadness, this is surprise. Really, though, emotions are far more layered and complex."

For example, two people might experience anger in markedly different ways, with one lashing out and the other beating himself up internally. Ditto happiness, sadness, and so on. One person can also experience different variations of a single larger emotion, such as fear.

"If you just think about the times you've been scared, you probably have your own kind of internal categorization of the types of fear," she said. "For instance, this is the 'fun' scary, and this is the 'oh shit I'm literally about to lose it' scary. You have that internal way of organizing."

To Kerr, the distinction between those two types of fear is an important one, and she believes the difference could be the key to treating phobias.

"One way to manage fear is by lessening the scare factor and combining it with or increasing the fun factor," she said, emphasizing that this is still only a theory. "For example, if you are really afraid of spiders, do something where you're engaging with them in an amusing, absurd, fun kind of way. Traditional exposure therapy is based on desensitization; you start with maybe a picture of a spider, and then maybe a stuffed animal of a spider, and you work up to the real thing. Our theory says no, start with a twenty-foot, massive animatronic spider that's so ridiculous that when you encounter it, you can't help but be like, 'Oh my gosh!' You have that startle response. You activate your fear response, but you're also laughing. You're basically adding some fun into the scary. Instead of trying to desensitize, you're making it absurd. A spoonful of sugar really can help the medicine go down."

In *Resident Evil*'s history, it's gone from one to the other. What inspired night terrors in 1996 is now a regular fixture in YouTube compilations of unintentionally funny video game moments. It still retains its capacity to frighten, but it's hard to imagine someone playing through it today and not finding the performances, character models, or some aspects of the design ridiculous. By Kerr's reasoning, *Resident Evil*'s campiness may actually make it a helpful tool for those who are looking to overcome their own severe reactions to horror.

When we do get scared, whoever we are, there are a few consistent things that happen in our bodies.

"A nice way of talking about it is that there are averages," Kerr said. "There's the average response that typically shows up as the sympathetic nervous system response, the fight-or-flight response which kicks our metabolism into high gear, the release of endorphins. We have all of these different chemical changes that are working to make our body very strong, very fast. That much looks consistent across people, across time, but it's not one size fits all. There's still lots of variation."

One notable, near-universal side effect of the fear response is panic.

"All of our attention, all of our resources, are going toward our body," Kerr continued. "There's not a lot going on in the area of our minds that is responsible for making critical, logical decisions. It's all going toward,

'Run! Flee! Fight! Do something!' It's very much a heightened state, and it's difficult to think rationally."

If you've ever criticized a horror character for fleeing into a basement or a blind alley, well, you were right; they were being idiots. But there is an actual, clinical explanation for their idiocy! As such, I am fully excused for the many times I fumbled desperately with the controller because a zombie scared me and I forgot how to shoot.

Knowing a little more about how our minds and bodies process fear, I wondered if the source of that fear made any difference. Was my reaction to being chased around a cramped room by a huge, venomous serpent any different, clinically speaking, than if I were being chased by the same thing in real life? To find out, I reached out to Sharnay Brown, an outpatient psychologist who holds a doctorate in clinical psychology.

"Our bodies physiologically react very similarly in both situations when the fear response is engaged," Brown told me. She listed examples, such as releases of adrenaline and cortisol ("the stress hormone"), the dilation of pupils, and blood rushing to our legs to carry us to safety. And that's just the beginning.

"Anything that is not needed for survival in that moment will shut down," Brown continued. "The digestive system shuts down, the reproductive organs shut down. Respiration increases. Heart rate increases. We'll sometimes have a tingling in our hands, and muscles will contract. Time can seem to slow down. People sometimes get tunnel vision. Whether it is a perceived threat or an actual threat, our brain can react in the same way."

There is, of course, one difference between guiding Jill through a house of horrors and attempting to escape one ourselves: the awareness that we can't actually come to physical harm.

"We are aware that we are not in actual danger through the use of the prefrontal cortex," she explained. "The prefrontal cortex helps to regulate the expression and suppression of fear through a number of mechanisms. We are able to have our fear system activated, so our amygdala and the limbic system sends the signal to the brain that says, 'I'm scared, this feels dangerous,' and our prefrontal cortex can help us distinguish and come in and say, 'This is a video game; we're not in actual danger.'"

If you ever thought horror was more enjoyable with friends, Brown is happy to prove it scientifically.

"Let's say someone starts to think, 'This is too real,'" she explained. "If they then look over at their friend who is laughing, that signal provides context to the stimulus that they're okay, that it's actually excitement, and maybe the level of fear was misperceived. We can actually quickly change from fear to excitement, because they're so similar within the body."

Kerr believes that the physical distance between ourselves and the creatures we encounter in *Resident Evil* allows us to immerse ourselves more fully in the experience. The fact that we can turn the game off and step away from the nightmare is key.

"It's that critical piece of control," she said. "Knowing that we can choose when we're going to engage allows us to more fully engage. It's called stressor controllability; knowing that it's all up to us allows us to be fully present. Otherwise, if it's an actual threat, we're focused on self-preservation. We have to know that we have a degree of agency to fully be present in a space and enjoy it."

In short, the knowledge that you're detached physically allows you to detach emotionally.

"Think about all the horror B-movies," she continued, "all the cheap, low-grade movies that are ridiculous, where you're like, 'I see the strings that are attached to the monster,' but you still jump and you still scream. What I think, based on my research, is that those elements allow us to engage in a more fully immersed way than we can when it's super real. When it's super real we are going to have our defenses up, but when we know it's campy and ridiculous, we just lean in. 'Okay, I'm going with it.' We let down our walls and make ourselves vulnerable in a good way, an entertaining way."

She shared an example from her days of designing haunted house scenes. What shattered suspension of disbelief wasn't a fake-looking pile of guts or an overacting vampire; it was a fish in a blender, with an invitation to guests to turn it on.

"Of course there was no blade inside the blender; it was more of a psychological kind of confrontation," she said. "And it pulled visitors out of the scene. They didn't buy it."

The fish was real and the blender was real, but the effect felt less real to visitors than any of the corpses and entrails that were obviously fake.

"They were fully willing to believe that the devil himself was going to condemn them to Hell or whatever," she explained. "They can believe a demon-possessed actor, but a blender with a fish in it? No. Things that are too real start us thinking, 'Wait a minute, are they really going to do this? No, they couldn't possibly go through however many goldfish a night. Oh my gosh, PETA would be so upset.'"

The closer something seems to plausibility, the more we question it. Now you have a perfect response whenever somebody asks why you don't question the melting Nazis in *Raiders of the Lost Ark* but take great issue with Indiana Jones surviving a nuclear blast in a refrigerator in *Kingdom of the Crystal Skull*. It's certainly why I'm okay with zombies rising from the dead while the reveal that Wesker faked *his* death feels like cheating.

"The prefrontal cortex in a way overrides the body's and mind's initial response," Brown said. "If you're watching a movie and something improbable happens, that can pull you completely out of the moment. Yet there's dragons flying around. It's interesting that those small little things pull us out of that arousal state, and instead engage the rational part of our minds."

Of course, that just made me wonder about *not* being able to detach. What if some particular game or film digs its fangs into us and refuses to let go? In short, is it possible to be scared to death?

"No," Brown said, instantly destroying my only excuse for not playing *Resident Evil 7* in virtual reality. "Generally, you are not going to die specifically from the emotion or the experience of fear."

"It's not going to be death by fear," Kerr explained further, "but it may be death by heart attack, brought on by hypertension or existing heart problems. Stress in our body is going to stress everything. If you have any underlying conditions, it really can intensify that."

For young children, though, horror can have genuinely severe consequences.

"In adults, our prefrontal cortex is fully developed," Brown said. "We are able to differentiate between real and imaginary. In children, the prefrontal cortex is not fully developed yet, so it's more difficult for them to tell the difference between trauma on the screen and trauma in real life. Their arousal part of the brain is active and has greater difficulty emotionally regulating itself, and that can easily overwhelm their understanding of what is safe and what is not."

This is why children often suffer nightmares after exposure to horror, while it's much less frequent in adults.

Fear is such a primal element of our emotional makeup that entertainment is not the only form of media that can exploit it. For every Joe Hill sending enjoyable chills down your spine, there's a Joseph McCarthy using fear to manipulate.

"This is where I started my career," Kerr told me. "I was focusing on the negative consequences of fear in society. The use of fearmongering. It's so effective because it taps into the very system that is responsible for our survival throughout the history of humans. It's been our threat response that has alerted us to danger, and so we've evolved to always pay attention to it, to put everything else on the back burner."

She explained that fear is a powerful motivator to action.

"You want to get somebody to do something? You scare them. But you also give them the solution," she said. "It's like the commercials from the 80s for home security systems. They'd show the evil burglar lurking around and the alarm going off, and so here's the solution to all of your concerns. In politics you see that same formula. 'You'd better be scared, but don't worry, I've got the answer.'"

Fortunately, we can stay vigilant about our own capacity to be manipulated.

"I tell my students that people need to understand their own threat response," Kerr said. "I tell them not to let other people hijack their fear response, or use fear to meet their own ends. We should always be making sure it is working for us, not being used by others to get us to do things. It's a retooling we have to do in modern society."

That would be a pretty dour end to the conversation, though, so I wanted to find out which horror movie gave the fear specialist nightmares as a kid. What corny, cheesy VHS rental scared the hell out of her and made her wish she'd never seen it?

"I don't think it was a movie," Kerr admitted. "It was the 'Thriller' video."

As other people's dreams were haunted by Michael Myers, Kerr's were haunted by Michael Jackson.

"I'll never forget!" she laughed. "I was walking down the stairs in my friend's house and it was on TV, and I was like, 'Oh! Oh my god! What is that?!'"

She chuckled as she remembered the effect the music video had on her.

"I watched the whole thing!" she said. "And then I had nightmares about Michael Jackson, and the zombies, and just that whole landscape."

Eventually she saw Jackson's other videos and her fear dissipated, but she still remembers that first horror experience today, and she remembers it with fondness.

That's the seductive contradiction of the horror genre: A game can upset us, terrorize us, and haunt the living shit out of us... and leave us with fond memories anyway.

THE LIVING DEAD GIRL

I SURVIVE, BUT MY FIGHT with Yawn leaves me badly hurt. No sooner do I leave the room than Jill grabs her head and slides down the wall, overcome by Yawn's venom. She passes out, and I just barely see someone step into view before the screen goes dark. When she wakes up in the save room, she's fully healed and cured of poison.

Barry rescued me. He gave me the acid rounds I needed to defeat Yawn, and then he carried me to safety when I nearly died. He's my mushmouthed guardian angel.

This is not an event everybody playing as Jill will experience. If you do well enough in the Yawn fight and avoid getting bitten, Jill will be just fine afterward. She'll have no need of rescue. In fact, as much as we all love Barry, Jill is fully capable of surviving the Spencer Mansion without his help. This stands in stark contrast to Chris, who at various points needs Rebecca to help him advance and bail him out of trouble.

One of the most notable illustrations of this difference comes when we enter the dormitory.

The dormitory is a small area just a short distance from the Spencer Mansion, designed as temporary housing for the Umbrella researchers.

It's cozier than the Spencer Mansion. There's a rec room with an abandoned game of pool, a still-lit pinball table, and empty beer bottles. There are sleeping quarters with private bathrooms. If it weren't for the gigantic spiders, mutant bees, and vines that keep reaching up through the floor to strangle me, it would be a pretty nice place.

As with the keeper's room, I find the zombified occupants shambling around, hungry for flesh. I have plenty of ammo for my handgun at this point. As with the keeper, I'm doing them a favor.

On one of the beds, I find the Plant 42 Report. Its sole entry claims to have been written four days after the accident. Taken with what we remember from the Keeper's Diary, that's May 15, 1998. It tells us that an experiment subject known as Plant 42 had an extreme reaction to something called the T-Virus. So extreme, in fact, that it's developed surprising intelligence.

Those tendrils reaching through holes to attack us? That's Plant 42, which has essentially seized the dormitory as its own. Its vines creep along the walls, and if we attempt to open the door to its room, we find that

Plant 42 is barricading the entrance, a behavior that the author of the Plant 42 Report believes is deliberate.

Plant 42 is the second boss fight, and Jill and Chris have very different experiences. (Perhaps you could call them branching paths.)

The original *Biohazard* explicitly labelled Chris's mode as HARD and Jill's as EASY, implying that the choice was nothing more than a difficulty select. I'd guess these labels were removed from *Resident Evil* to prevent someone from finishing the game as one character and assuming there's no reason to replay it as the other.

In actuality, each character learns and experiences things that the other does not. Chris, for example, learns more about Umbrella's involvement in the disaster than Jill does, and Jill learns of Barry's involvement in the coverup. To get the full story, it's necessary to play as both.

Both Chris and Jill collect the V-JOLT Report when sneaking into Plant 42's room, which offers an enticing option. "In our calculation," it reads, "it will take less than 5 seconds to destroy Plant 42 if we put the 'V-JOLT' directly on the root."

Jill can pop into the nearby chemical storeroom, whip up a batch, dump it on the roots, and weaken Plant 42 before she even fights it.

Chris, by contrast, can't do jack shit. He doesn't know how to mix chemicals and can't even try. Instead, he attempts to take on Plant 42 with firepower alone, and ends up snagged helpless in its vines. Rebecca finds him and offers her help. (The voice acting in this scene is a cheesy highlight, from Chris referring to herbicide as a "potion" to Rebecca's advice: "Chris! Don't die!") We then gain control of Rebecca to mix the V-JOLT.

Something similar happens when Chris encounters Richard: His inability to understand basic chemistry means it's up to us to guide Rebecca to the serum while Chris stays behind like a lump.

Jill's mode isn't easier because the game is going easier on her; Jill's mode is easier because she's more competent. The Spencer Mansion is a large, complex game of chess, and Chris is equipped to do little more than flip the board.

While the game's dialogue and vocal performances make every character sound like they aged out of the school system, Jill demonstrates her intelligence through her abilities, whether picking locks, mixing chemicals, or playing the piano. Through the years, I've mainly played as Jill because it's easier, sure, but I also liked her more. She was a lone spark of competence among the meatheads.

Jill's competence was especially refreshing in the mid-90s, the same era in which *Dead or Alive* gave us "jiggle physics," *Policenauts* included animated groping as an option for engaging with female characters, and, of course, *Tomb Raider* introduced the world to Lara Croft.

Croft has all the makings of a strong female character. She's an adventurer. She has no need of anyone else to protect her. She's competent and self-reliant.

She was also immediately sexualized. The marketing blitz for the game forced this image; consumers were made to see Lara Croft as a sex object. Her polygonal video game model "posed" topless for *Loaded* magazine. She appeared topless on the cover of *Next Generation*, parodying the famous *Rolling Stone* cover featuring Janet Jackson and a pair of eager male hands. (Duke Nukem filled that role for *Next Generation*.) *Playboy* even featured a completely nude Lara Croft photo spread.

Jill represented a welcome alternative. She was an officer of the law. She was a survivor. She contributed more to STARS and to the mission than anyone else in the game. Ditto Rebecca, the youngest member of STARS, and the only Bravo to live through the night. Her male colleagues perished, but she was knowledgeable, resourceful, and capable enough to make it out alive.

After applying the V-JOLT, Plant 42 is a pushover. A few shots from the bazooka kill it easily, and I'm free to take a key from the fireplace. On my way back, however, I bump into Wesker, all sunglasses and swagger as though he has nothing to account for.

He instructs me to return to the mansion without him. He doesn't ask about Barry. He doesn't mention Chris. He doesn't tell me how he made it into the dormitory or where he's going next.

As quickly as I found him, I'm left alone again, this time with even more questions.

Strange behavior for someone who should be deeply concerned for the safety of his team.

It's a good thing Jill can watch out for herself, because her commanding officer sure doesn't seem interested in doing it.

IT FOLLOWS

THOUGH I HAVE FAR LESS experience with it, this second half of the game does so many things so perfectly that I'm still impressed by how well it's constructed.

Now that I have the key Plant 42 was guarding, nothing in the Spencer Mansion is closed off to me. This offers no kind of relief, however; as the number of secrets held by the game decreases, the danger ramps up to compensate.

I'm barely back inside the mansion proper before I see the same environment I just left through some unidentified creature's eyes. It bounds nimbly to the mansion in something like a quarter of the time it took me to jog back. A green hand reaches for the door, and I regain control, now face to face with this new monster. It may look like a polygonal Battletoad, but the threat it poses is real.

This is a hunter. It is now our main threat.

Hunters are much faster and stronger than zombies. They have long claws, which allow them to perform an instant-kill move. Those claws also make them unnerving as hell; I hear them clicking along the wooden floors before I know where they are. While zombie moans served a similar purpose, I at least had a fighting chance of getting away if one caught me. The hunters are both more likely to get the drop on me and less likely to let me get away alive.

They've also infested rooms I've previously cleared. Whatever few safe spaces I'd carved out for myself are gone.

It's an effective way to reintroduce horror to the areas we thought we knew, and it tests our ability to react to danger in a way earlier enemies did not. *Resident Evil* gave us the time and space necessary to familiarize ourselves with the many passages through the maze-like Spencer Mansion, and the hunters punish those who still need to take the time to find an exit.

The game isn't all cruelty at this point. Outside the second save room, I find a note from Barry. He left me some goodies, including ammo and a can of first aid spray. It's a rare moment of true generosity in *Resident Evil*.

I soon bump into him in another room, where he helps me examine a mysterious hole in the floor.

> BARRY: How about going down to check by yourself? I have a rope here.

> JILL: Oh, do you? Well then I'll try to go down using the rope.

Good to know *Resident Evil* hasn't lost its flair for dialogue in the homestretch.

In fact, the further I get into *Resident Evil*, the more I appreciate just how well-formed it is. I keep finding new ways to understand and appreciate it. I think about it. I read about it. I watch movies based on it. In my career as a games journalist, I'd reference it frequently. Now I'm writing this book about it.

I was far from the only one who fell under *Resident Evil*'s spell, and also far from the only one who struggled to articulate why. In fact, Capcom itself seemed to struggle to find ways to convey its difficult charms.

On August 31, 1995, Capcom distributed an astonishingly inaccurate press release, making it rather easy to identify the critics who didn't play much of the game. These reviewers refer to nonexistent locations such as a tower and a graveyard. They claim the objective is to find the "hidden helicopter." They parrot the press release's erroneous list of items: "crossbows, bazookas, chainsaws, shotguns, fire extinguishers, explosive cans of gasoline, knives, hammers, axes, torches, matches, medicine, and maps." If you haven't played *Resident Evil* in a while, it might be fun to see if you can remember which of those things actually appeared in the game.

The press release does, at least, put the game's cinematic ambitions front and center, calling *Resident Evil* the first game to capture "the kind of action and drama that directors like John Carpenter, Alfred Hitchcock, or Sam Raimi have been able to achieve on film."

Interestingly, as the press release struggles to define *Resident Evil*'s genre, it doesn't use the game's own description of survival horror. Instead, it's described as "a third-person perspective action game with elements of role-playing and puzzle solving," which we can all agree is not quite as catchy.

I don't know why Capcom would have marketed the game with inaccurate information. It's possible that it was a deliberate attempt to mislead, to make the game sound more exciting than it was, but the differences only hint toward a slightly different shade of excitement. Some player somewhere might personally think it would be more fun to fight zombies with a crossbow in a graveyard, but is that an inherently more exciting proposition than fighting them with a bazooka in the catacombs? It's more likely the marketing team got a hold of some outdated design documents and the developers never let them know that anything had changed.

The details of the press release weren't the only way Capcom confused journalists. Writing for *The Charleston Gazette*, Douglas Imbrogno recounts receiving a package in the mail. "The cardboard box had a huge, bloodshot eye decorating its cover," he writes. It contained a number of goodies, and the main attraction was "an advance release of the latest and goriest of all video games, at least for this month."

Critics and journalists are used to receiving goodies promoting new and upcoming releases. Keychains, stickers, hats, coffee mugs. To promote *Resident Evil*, Imbrogno received "one oily-black, high-top army boot with thick, heavy rubber soles."

Never having played *Resident Evil*, he was baffled. Having played *Resident Evil* many times, I'm just as baffled.

List the things that come to mind when you think about *Resident Evil*. The Umbrella logo. The STARS insignia. A green herb. Jill's beret. Forest Speyer's entrails. A boot wouldn't make your top 100.

"All last week across America," Imbrogno wrote, "editors opened their *Resident Evil* kits, pulled out the army boot, looked at it for 10 seconds, maybe said 'Hey, look at this,' to a nearby person. Then tens of thousands of 'THUDS!' resounded across the land as editors tossed the boots into trash cans. Those thousands of boots will sit around in landfills for several centuries. They might decompose by, say, the return of Comet Hyakutake, due back in 18,000 years."

Other reviewers did actually play the game, but didn't necessarily understand any better how to talk about it.

In an April 1996 issue of the Zanesville, Ohio newspaper *The Times Recorder*, reviewer Tom Brown spends roughly half of his *Resident Evil* review describing his own apartment. He barely talks about the game; and when he does, he resorts to vague language such as "body movements," "surprises," and "rooms." Reading the review may actually make you understand *Resident Evil* less. He mentions two enemy types and none of the puzzles, which leads me to believe he played for around an hour. He does, however, claim to have enjoyed it.

"This particular interactive game seems very real," he says, causing me to wonder how a game could be anything other than interactive. "I can't wait to attempt it again… in the light of day, of course."

It's a nice thought, but evidently he could at least wait until after he'd finished reviewing it.[13]

Just about every critic, though, conceded at least some degree of fascination. A month after Brown's review, Roy Bassave of the *Miami Herald* only begrudgingly conceded that, "the game does have some redeeming qualities," namely its puzzles, level of detail, and camera angles. When it comes to the latter, he assumes that players are viewing the action through "hidden cameras placed throughout the

13 This was actually a dual review with the Steve Martin film *Sgt. Bilko*. I wonder if *Alone in the Dark* ever got reviewed alongside *Rock-a-Doodle*.

mansion," something in no way supported by the game itself, but which illustrates a critic making a good-faith attempt to communicate the unique feel of the game and falling into the language of film.

Also interesting is the lengthy warning to parents with which he ends his review: "This game is designed for adults. [...] The stuff of nightmares, *Resident Evil* is not appropriate for kids under 17."

The fact that critics would have had to issue such direct caution speaks volumes. The social understanding at that time was that video games were for children. *Resident Evil* represents a turning point in that mindset; it was one of the first games that definitely wasn't for young ones to kill time with before church.

A few critics clearly understood the impact the game was destined to have. A glowing review from Tom Ham for the *Washington Post* cautions players that, in spite of its clunkiness, *Resident Evil* is "a truly terrifying experience that sucks you in and won't let you up for air."

He compliments the game for maintaining "nearly constant" suspense. He calls the animations the best he's seen. He lavishes praise on the sound design. "You hear everything," he writes, "from the faint music of a piano playing behind a door, to crickets chirping outside, to the clicking of the gun when you're out of bullets."

He then lists weapons that are actually in the game. Imagine that.

"With a little practice you'll find yourself playing one of the best video games ever produced," he says. "I know it's early, but this just may be the Game of the Year."[14]

Many critics didn't know what to make of this strange, creepy new game, and simply repeated Capcom's marketing copy. Others were turned off by the gore. A few, like Ham, saw a profound development in the medium.

Nobody, it seems, believed it was destined to fail, myself included, however much I resented its difficulty, its cruelty, and the joy it took in scaring the living shit out of me. I hated it and I couldn't get enough of it. I kept coming back to it, long before I understood how—and why—to appreciate it. That's what allowed it to endure, even as its fans and critics and developer floundered for ways to explain what the damned thing was.

Effective horror sticks. It resonates. It doesn't just spook; it worms its way into our psyches and torments us from within. It makes us see and process the world differently than we normally would. It makes us afraid to pick up hitchhikers. It makes us reluctant to dangle our feet off the edges of our beds. It makes us see shapes in the shadows. It makes us assign motive to noises in the night. It rewires our brains. It refuses to let us escape. It gives us nightmares to prevent even sleep from

---

14 Shed a tear for Ham's colleague Steve Marsh, who reviewed *Nester's Funky Bowling* for the same issue.

offering release, something Wes Craven immortalized in a literal sense with 1984's *A Nightmare on Elm Street.*

I have a friend who told me that he couldn't sleep in the same room as the box *Resident Evil* came in; he had to move it out of his bedroom every night. Another fan told me he played it around age ten. He lived in Norway and, being under eighteen, wasn't technically allowed to buy the game. He and a friend convinced an adult to buy it on their behalf, and they played all night. He learned the next morning that his friend suffered nightmares so severe that his mother threw the game away.

Resident Evil's ability to haunt its players has even worked its way into the cultural consciousness, notably driving an episode of *Spaced* in which Simon Pegg's character stays up all night playing *Resident Evil 2* and suffers waking nightmares as a result. This episode inspired Pegg and director Edgar Wright to create *Shaun of the Dead*, so if you enjoyed that movie, you have *Resident Evil* to thank.

THEY CAME
FROM WITHIN

I DON'T REMEMBER HOW OLD I was the first time I saw the creaky old mansion doors in the loading screens replaced by stainless steel ones, priceless antiques replaced by sterile medical equipment, or grand pianos replaced by computer keyboards, but it was a great "holy shit" moment.

I thought I was in one kind of story. I was in a different one entirely.

The loading screens in *Resident Evil* are among its most memorable features. Against a black screen you watch a short animation of a door or a staircase or a lift, you hear the game disc spin like the wheel of fortune, and you grit your teeth, wondering if the room you're stepping into is a little more or a lot less safe than the one you just left.

During these moments, before I had the Spencer Mansion more or less memorized, the anticipation was close to unbearable. The door could open on a save room or thrust me into a crowd of hungry zombies. The slow movements of the protagonists meant that I had to see, absorb, and process my new environment the moment it winked into existence and decide immediately on a course of action. Nearly always I'd choose the wrong one. That was part of the fun.

As I enter the lab proper, the significant change in scenery reflected in the loading screens still manages to fill me with uneasiness.

It's unlikely to be much of a surprise to players today, but the fact that the game extended beyond the mansion was positively mind-blowing in 1996. The mansion was dangerous, but given enough time and exploration, I could learn its secrets. I could gauge my progress by the decreasing number of locked doors. Now there was no such way to measure things. How much more of the game *was* there?

This is also where we lose the ability to see the monsters of *Resident Evil* as an external threat.

However many notes we found in the mansion, whatever we might have suspected about the source of all this horror, we concentrated mostly on the immediate danger, on the monster around the corner, on the fight to just stay alive. We could let the real monsters—the human beings who worked in a formalized effort to bring this nightmare to life—stay somewhere in the shadows.

In this last area, the lab, we don't have that option. The Spencer Mansion looks like it could be the home of some ancient evil, but the lab is too new, too advanced, too clean for that. This is a recent evil.

Stephen King, in his 1981 book *Danse Macabre*, observed that all horror can be divided between works in which the monster is external and works in which the monster is internal.

Most monster movies and slasher films feature an external threat, a beast or presence that pursues, menaces, destroys. The heroes nearly always have a clear objective: Escape or defeat that threat. The Predator is an external threat, as is Dracula, as is Godzilla.

In the internal set, we have psychological horror: stories of madness, meditations on innate evil. There may not be any clear objective for the protagonists to accomplish in these stories, and there may not even be any heroes. "The Tell-Tale Heart" illustrates this kind of horror well. There is indeed a murderer in Edgar Allan Poe's story, but the horror comes in the form of hallucinations brought on by his overwhelming guilt. Robert Louis Stevenson's *The Strange Case of Dr. Jekyll and Mr. Hyde* is probably the most famous example, with the conflict between the amiable Jekyll and cruel Hyde playing out internally. Both halves of the same man's personality vie for power, with the latter assuming greater and greater control as the story progresses.

Also, King happens to describe this kind of horror as "inside evil." The close similarity between that phrase and "Resident Evil" is clearly a coincidence, but a damned interesting one.[15]

Sometimes stories can straddle the line between internal and external horror. Other times, a story that starts as one gradually becomes the other. My favorite example is "The Monsters Are Due on Maple Street," a penetrating episode of *The Twilight Zone* in which neighbors gradually convince themselves that they are in danger from aliens and turn on each other, accuse each other, fight each other. They think they are in a story in which the monster is external while we at home come to understand, with increasing horror, that they are not.[16] There is also 1964's *The Last Man on Earth*, in which Vincent Price spends his time hunting the undead, only to realize too late that he's actually been murdering other survivors.

---

15 Mikami naming his 2014 horror game *The Evil Within* was just as clearly not a coincidence.

16 To be fair, there actually are "monsters" in the traditional sense involved, but they don't need to do anything other than introduce uncertainty to the humans. As one explains to the other at the episode's end, "They pick the most dangerous enemy they can find, and it's themselves. All we need do is sit back and watch."

Most of *Resident Evil* feels like external horror. Stepping into the lab, though, we can no longer convince ourselves that's the case. The zombies and hunters and angry plants are still scary, but suddenly they're just symptoms. The *real* monster is the part of us that would accept money to create bioorganic weapons, that would kill innocent people for the sake of research, that would willfully choose to never question orders.

It's here—after solving more puzzles, digging through more logs, pulling out the magnum for the new monkey-like chimera enemy—that I find Barry again.

BARRY: Jill, you're here too?

JILL: Yes. You're here too?

These two were made for each other.

And then, at last, I come face to face with Wesker. He's standing in a tight corridor, ready for me. Barry—sweet doofus Barry—puts his gun to my head. Wesker explains his orders, which indeed match what we learned from the security memo earlier.

JILL: So you're a slave of Umbrella now, along with these virus monsters!

WESKER: I think you misunderstand me, Jill. To me, the monsters you mentioned

mean nothing. I'm going to burn all of
them together, with this entire laboratory.
I must complete my mission, as ordered by
Umbrella.

To recap, Jill was wrong to assume Wesker was a
slave of Umbrella... because he's actually doing whatever
they tell him to do.

We also learn that Barry is only cooperating with
him—and disposing of evidence on his behalf—to
ensure the safety of his wife and two daughters, whom
Wesker has kidnapped.[17]

Wesker starts to lead me into a room to meet the
fruit of the T-Virus research: Tyrant.

This monster, whatever it is, is the culmination of
every one of these hideous experiments. Wesker will
collect his battle data and eliminate me at the same time.
Then he'll blow up the mansion, report to Umbrella,
and retire on a beach somewhere. Evil will prevail.

But then Barry—loveable idiot Barry—pistol whips
him from behind, putting the good guys back in control.

---

17 I always took this as gospel, but in *The Umbrella
Conspiracy*, the official novelization of the game, author
S.D. Perry interprets this as a bluff on Wesker's part: Barry's
family is safe and the poor guy doesn't know it. I prefer
Perry's take, which feels even more theatrically cruel.

We celebrate, of course, by sputtering nonsense at each other.

> BARRY: Do you think we could see Tyrant now?

> JILL: Barry, you're so optimistic.

Words used to mean things. Really, they did.

The next scene plays out differently depending upon the protagonist and various choices made along the way. The way it plays out for me here sees Barry dopily tapping away at a computer keyboard, accidentally releasing Tyrant instead of killing it. In other versions—such as when playing as Chris, or if we as Jill treated Barry badly enough that he doesn't show up to help us—Tyrant is deliberately released by Wesker. In this case, Tyrant immediately attacks and kills Wesker, echoing the death of Victor Frankenstein at the hands of his own monstrous creation in Mary Shelley's novel.

Either way we have our next boss fight here, and there isn't much to it. Tyrant is a massive humanoid of incredible strength, but he's also fairly slow, and lab equipment in the middle of the room makes it easy to keep our distance from him. A few shots from the magnum or the bazooka is all it takes to lay him out, further reinforcing the idea that the external evil isn't the problem. We can kill monsters. We can defeat Wesker. We can blow up the mansion.

But that's not what matters. What matters is that evil exists in enough of us that this cycle will repeat, again and again, forever.

We each have a price, and there will always be an Umbrella willing to pay it.

A BLACK VEIL FOR LISA

BARRY AND I EXIT TYRANT'S arena and we're greeted by the howling blasts of an alarm. Wesker's body is gone. Something is happening, and thankfully we can duck into the final save room before we have to find out what it is.

As much evidence as we find of Umbrella's atrocities, we don't learn about their most heinous one in the original game.

Instead, *Resident Evil*'s last, best story was introduced in the 2002 GameCube remake, which saw the *Resident Evil* experience rebuilt from the ground up. As tempting as it may be to grumble about companies fiddling with certified classics, this newer version of *Resident Evil*—often referred to as *REmake* by fans, and I admit the wordplay is irresistible—leaves little room for complaint.

REmake had its work cut out for it. Returning director Mikami knew that if he wanted to scare players, he couldn't simply put new textures on old enemies or ratchet up the gore. Instead, he'd have to surprise them, somehow, all over again.

REmake turned out to be a masterclass in misdirection and subverted expectations. It's exactly the game you remember until it isn't.

Replaying *REmake* as Jill for comparison, things start off familiarly enough, and after a much more detailed version of that slow, iconic turn, I lead the first zombie back to Barry, who shoots it for me. As we're about to head back to the foyer to report to Wesker, though, I hear an agonized groan, followed by the sound of creaking hinges. The camera shifts to the door next to the fireplace just as it closes. The same door I led the zombie through.

I head back that way. Lightning crashes. The zombie's blood is still there, but its body is not.

It's an important moment. In *REmake*, zombies don't stop being threats just because you killed them. A note you find in the first save room explains that they aren't truly dead unless you destroy the head or burn the body. Your unseen benefactor leaves some kerosene for you; it's up to you to find a lighter.[18] Ignore his advice and any zombie you kill will rise again, faster, stronger, and much more aggressive.

---

18 Unless you play as Chris, whose canonical smoking habit means he already has one.

REmake offers a sense of familiarity just to yank it out from under you. The moment you make it to That Hallway, you recognize it. You know what's going to come crashing through those windows. No player of the original game could possibly have forgotten.

And so you brace. You tense. You walk down the hall, as you must, and you steel yourself. You may still jump, but you're *ready*.

The window cracks, but doesn't break.

The dogs threw themselves against the glass, and the glass held.

You're safe.

Until, of course, you come back to the hallway later and they make a second, more successful attempt at their dramatic entrance.

REmake could have just enhanced the visuals, found some new voice actors, and updated the controls. Instead, Mikami and Capcom gave fans a reimagining that remained true to their memories while building upon them in genuinely impressive ways.

It also added a character to the story, and far from just being "extra content," she stands to this day as the series's greatest achievement. Few characters in all of gaming have left as large an impression on me as Lisa Trevor.

Through journals, *REmake* introduces the brains behind the Spencer Mansion: brilliant architect George Trevor. Known for his complex designs and secret passageways, George was hired to design the Spencer Mansion, which would become a front for Umbrella's bioweapon program. As far as he was aware, the project was just a thrilling opportunity to let his imagination run wild with unlimited funding from Umbrella's founder, the wealthy Oswell Spencer. It's safe to assume his wife, Jessica, and his fourteen-year-old daughter, Lisa, were thrilled for him as well.

It wasn't until it was far too late that George realized what was happening. "There are only two people that know the secret of this mansion," we read in his journal. "If they kill me, Sir Spencer will be the only person that knows the secret."

To Spencer, George is simply a loose end, and Umbrella disposes of him accordingly. His wife and daughter, though, are more than that. They are valuable test subjects.

Umbrella researchers inject them with something called the Progenitor Virus. Jessica receives Type A, and her body rejects it. She plans to escape with Lisa, but the researchers have no further use for her, and she is killed.

Lisa receives Type B, and her body accepts it. The researchers keep her alive and observe her progress.

As unfortunate as George and Jessica were, they were far luckier than their daughter. Lisa was damned not by her father's crimes, but by his talents. There's no reason to see George as a greedy man, or an evil man, or even a foolish man. He simply had the misfortune to be useful to a deeply terrible person.

It's a more realistic kind of horror than it might at first seem. We could remove the Progenitor Virus from the equation and be left with a story of abduction, captivity, and relentless cruelty that robs a child not of her life but of her freedom, dignity, and future.

When STARS arrives in 1998, Lisa is still alive. She's spent 31 years in captivity, being experimented upon, observed, tortured—treated like an animal. She's clothed only in a rotting hospital gown. Her wrists are permanently bound by wooden shackles.

I heard her moaning behind an early, locked door as I replayed *REmake*—later revealed to lead to her mother's tomb—and immediately remembered so much about her.

Lisa is the strongest, most resilient monster in the game, and she's also the most helpless. Whatever empathy you might potentially feel for a zombified researcher or a mutated dog is balanced at least somewhat by the fact that you can kill them, freeing them from their misery. Lisa can't be killed. Immortality is her curse.

Around halfway through *REmake*, I find a new outdoor area that leads to a cabin. Inside, the fireplace burns. Somebody's been here. I look for the occupant, but she finds me.

Lisa is a difficult sight to behold. She's sickly, bony, hunched over. Her face is hidden behind a mask of baggy flesh. She shuffles rather than walks, every movement accompanied by howls of agony. She's covered in writhing veins and hideous mutations. She's beyond reasoning with. Get too close and she'll clobber you with her heavy shackles. Linger too long and she will hunt you down.

You can only run. You can only flee. You can only shut your eyes and wish you could forget what you've seen. You pity her and fear her in equal measure. She's both pathetic and terrifying.

Much later I encounter her beneath the mansion. She hobbles after me as I sprint from room to room, keeping my distance, trying to find a way out. Eventually I see a ladder. I climb it and find myself right back in her cabin, where I first encountered her. In fleeing her, I circled right back to where she lives. It's a great surprise, and it reinforces the feeling that she's always there... that you're never as far from her as you wish you were.

Lisa is living evidence of how inhuman Umbrella's experiments really are. By gradually revealing her tragedy, by drilling down so deeply into what happened to her, *REmake* manages to improve on the horror of the original game.

We learn in a journal—even in the remake, epistolary storytelling is one of *Resident Evil*'s best features—that

Umbrella had female researchers pose as Jessica in an attempt to keep the increasingly monstrous Lisa calm enough that they could study the progress of the virus incubating in her. They did not just strip her of humanity, but they impersonated her mother—the mother they themselves murdered—to keep her from lashing out at them.

Umbrella is fully aware of its own cruelty. Victims such as George, Jessica, and Lisa don't just happen to get caught in the gears of its dreadful machinery; the machine is designed to crush them. It's not an unfortunate quirk of fate that the researchers stare for hours every day into the eyes of the little girl whose life they robbed from her. It's not a regrettable accident that the scientists reluctantly decide to roll with because they feel their research is just that important.

No. Their plan all along was to ruin lives, over and over, until they managed to find a victim whose life would be ruined in precisely the right way, so they could then use that research to ruin more lives.

Lisa's story is disturbing and horrifying, and told with impressive restraint. Resident Evil has often been bigger, but it's never been better.

You can't kill Lisa. You can't grant her rest. You can't take her pain away. You're a well-armed, good-looking American… but you can't be her hero.

The closest thing you can do is open Jessica's casket, at which point the girl grabs her mother's skull and retreats into the depths of the estate. You can call this closure if you must.

You can call it whatever you like. It doesn't change anything.

FEAR NO EVIL

IT ISN'T NECESSARY TO DO SO, but we can explore the area to find Wesker's body, torn apart by chimeras. Before he died, he found his way to a computer terminal and initiated the detonation of the Spencer Mansion. It's a good thing he told us he's not a slave of Umbrella, because there's no way we would have drawn that conclusion otherwise.

If we collected three disks during the game, we can use them to release the other protagonist from a locked cell before we flee the estate. The decision determines who gets to go home tonight.

Resident Evil works hard at this stage to overwhelm us with anxiety. The alarms blare, Brad radios us to say that he's returning but that his helicopter is running out of fuel, and a three-minute timer on the screen begins ticking rapidly down toward detonation. What's more, once I do escape the lab, I find that Tyrant has survived and followed me to the helipad.

Time slips away as I grapple with Tyrant, am struck repeatedly by him, and pray that my shots are doing any kind of damage to him. He was a wimp before, but in this refight he lives up to his promised brutality. No matter how much lead I pump into him, he just keeps coming.

The clock ticks down. The helicopter above runs lower and lower on fuel. I consume healing item after healing item while Tyrant hasn't even broken a sweat.

But here's a secret: Mikami is only toying with us.

Just when things are at their bleakest, with almost no time to spare, Brad drops a rocket launcher and a ridiculous line of dialogue.

> BRAD: Kill that monster! You're our
> Amazon, Jill!

I blow that motherfucker to bits.

Mikami gives us a Hollywood action ending, with closeups from three different angles of Tyrant exploding into singed meat. Our director just wanted to see me get smacked around a bit before he gave me the tool I needed to succeed.

The danger is neither as real nor as time-sensitive as we were led to believe. Once you realize that, *Resident Evil*'s final sequence, however thrilling it can still be, isn't nearly as scary as it was on the first playthrough.

In fact, this is a sentiment I heard often while interviewing sources for this book. People would talk wistfully about how much the game terrified them… at the time.

Sometimes explicitly, other times implicitly, their conclusion was that *Resident Evil* isn't as scary today as it was in 1996.

In the first *Simpsons* Halloween special, Bart and Lisa share spooky stories, each attempting to frighten the other. Lisa brings out the literary big guns: Poe's "The Raven." Bart, however, is unmoved.

"That wasn't scary," he tells her. "Not even for a poem."

"It was written in 1845," she muses. "Maybe people were easier to scare."

"Like *Friday the 13th* part one," he agrees. "It's pretty tame by today's standards."

There's truth to Bart's joke. "The Raven" was nearly 150 years old by the time Lisa shared it with her older brother, and it had lost at least some of its power to shock. But *Friday the 13th* was released in 1980, only ten years before this episode. In that time, *Friday the 13th* aged just as much. As much as I love the game, I'd be lying if I said the years between 1996 and 2020 have been any kinder to *Resident Evil*.

Part of the reason *Resident Evil* won't feel as scary today is that we're familiar with it, whether through the game itself, its remake, its sequels, or any number of the games it inspired (such as *Silent Hill*, which took as much from *Resident Evil* as *Resident Evil* took from *Alone in the Dark*).

For horror to succeed, it needs to be unexpected. Lovecraft traced this fact back to the dawn of humanity. "Man's first instincts and emotions formed his response to the environment in which he found himself," he wrote. He discussed our ancestors developing feelings of pleasure and pain, and understanding the world around them through these lenses. "The unknown, being likewise the unpredictable, became for our primitive forefathers a terrible and omnipotent source of boons and calamities visited upon mankind for cryptic and wholly extra-terrestrial reasons, and thus clearly belonging to spheres of existence whereof we know nothing and wherein we have no part."

In short: Holy shit is the unknown scary.

We understand the universe better than our primitive forefathers did, but we still approach it, as individuals, in much the same way. We figure out what brings us pleasure, what brings us pain. We adjust our behaviors so that, ultimately, we can have more of the things we like and fewer of the things we don't.

But what of the things we don't know? The things we don't understand? Whether in the basement or lurking in the shadows or locked away inside our own minds? We don't know—and can't know—whether or not to steer away from them, or even how, because we don't know what they *are*.

That's where horror lives.

In *Danse Macabre*, Stephen King shared what he learned from William F. Nolan—author and screenwriter with credits from *Logan's Run* to *Trilogy of Terror*—at the World Fantasy Convention in 1979.

Nolan spoke of a hypothetical creature lurking behind a door. The door opens and the audience sees a ten-foot-tall bug. Perhaps it scares them, but there's a sense of relief. Until the door opened, the audience was afraid it might be a 100-foot-tall bug. Of course, had the door opened to reveal a 100-foot-tall bug, the audience would still be relieved because they were afraid the bug might be 1,000 feet tall.

The observable horror of the known can never measure up to the implicit horror of the unknown. Whatever we think might be behind that door is scarier than whatever *is* behind that door.

Every work of horror must ultimately reveal what's behind the door, at least to some degree. Smart horror—effective, chilling horror—conjures up monsters in the viewer's head and lets him or her spend as much time with them as possible. Once we see the bug, there's a sense of relief. Perhaps it scares us and perhaps it does not, but seeing it relieves us of the dread of anticipation.

I came nowhere near finishing *Resident Evil* with Michael and Dave, but subsequent playthroughs went more smoothly. I developed the presence of mind and calmer nerves required to get a little further each time. I knew the bug was ten feet tall. It was still dangerous, but I at least knew it wasn't going to get any bigger.

New rooms revealed new horrors, keeping the game lively and scary and thrilling, but every door opened to reveal how tall its own bug was, too. The next time through, I'd know.

In a 2016 discussion with Jason Bailey for Flavorwire, our friend the sociologist Margee Kerr put it directly: "Fundamentally, our fear is an error in our prediction system. [It's the disparity between] our ability to know what we are expecting to happen, and what actually happens. And when those things don't match up, we get scared." The unspoken corollary is that when we do expect what happens, we don't get scared.

Resident Evil as a series is rife with examples of effective horror, but each game threw open more doors to reveal the ten-foot-tall bugs behind them.

In the first game, we learned relatively little. There was a spooky mansion, we confronted a traitor, we uncovered the secrets of the underground lab, and we escaped. *Resident Evil 2* taught us quite a bit more, letting us learn about the Raccoon City Police Department— the parent organization of STARS—and brought us inside Umbrella, where we met its researchers. *Resident Evil 3* further broadened the scope of Raccoon City, and *Resident Evil – Code: Veronica* introduced the concept of more Umbrella facilities operating around the world.

Later games introduced new protagonists, pulled characters into different alliances and agencies and institutions, split Umbrella into various subsidiaries with their own motives—including Blue Umbrella, which is on the side of good, at least for now—introduced similar but not-directly-related outbreaks of similar but not-directly-related viruses... and, well, things got a bit unwieldy. This is without even dipping into the prequels and spinoffs and subseries, each of which shines its torch into yet another corner of what was once the darkness. What terrified us in the shadows flounders in the light.

All horror franchises are doomed to diminishing returns by sheer virtue of the fact that the central threat has to keep coming back or the core spectacle needs to outdo itself. We're more than willing to believe in Freddy Kreuger in the first *A Nightmare on Elm Street*, but it doesn't take long for the pattern to become established and the horror to drain from the endlessly repeating cycle.

Dracula once kept children awake in terror. Now he teaches them to count and sells them chocolate cereal. It's sometimes difficult to step back and realize what an enormous change this represents. By way of analogy, imagine an educational program starring Jigsaw from the Saw series. Perhaps children escape his traps using their knowledge of colors and shapes. Or imagine a brand of fruit snack using an animated Leatherface as a mascot. (Fruit-Leather Face?) That's exactly as absurd as what a century of familiarity did to Dracula. As I once heard the poet Stephen Dunn observe, he never thought there could one day be a band called The Dead Kennedys.

So, what can horror do to avoid this? Relatively little. Which, I think, is a decent argument for constructing horror as a series of isolated experiences rather than ongoing ones. A few examples of triumphs do suggest themselves, though, most notably Sam Raimi shepherding his Evil Dead franchise from a 1981 work of horror with minor comic elements through 1992's *Army of Darkness*, a work of comedy with minor horror elements. By leaning less on fear, the question of deflated horror becomes moot. We may know the bug is ten feet tall, but we didn't expect to see it get hit with a banana cream pie.

Resident Evil does seem to realize it's given too much away. 2017's *Resident Evil 7* broke the series back down to its core experience. It discarded the overcomplicated lore and told a simpler, isolated tale that was related to the larger series but functioned on its own. *Resident Evil 7* let the darkness back in and tipped the balance back toward the unknown.

You knew nothing more heading into the Baker House than you did the first time you stepped into the Spencer Mansion. The door had been closed again. Maybe the bug was still ten feet tall. For the first time in two decades, though, it was again possible for it to be 100 feet tall.

In horror, that possibility is enough.

REFLECTIONS IN BLACK

I'M REWARDED FOR OBLITERATING TYRANT with a final live-action scene. Jill, Barry, and Chris are in the helicopter. Brad is flying them home. Dawn breaks. The horror recedes. From above I watch the Spencer Mansion blow itself to Hell.

Barry checks his guns. Chris sighs with relief. Jill rests her head on his shoulder.

They're still processing. Reflecting. Grasping to understand.

I grew up hating horror. I didn't think it was interesting or fun. When my classmates talked about who would win in a fight between Freddy and Jason, I faked my way through participation. At slumber parties where my friends would suggest watching *Pumpkinhead* or *C.H.U.D.* or *My Bloody Valentine*—movies whose names alone sounded scary enough—I'd pretend to be asleep and try to actually fall asleep before I would hear them watching it.

I liked comedies. I liked cartoons. I liked fun things and silly things. I did not like horror. I didn't think there was any real love or craftsmanship behind it. As with the too-bloody ceramic Jesus with his crown of thorns that my grandparents owned, I was supposed to get something out of it, but all I felt was repulsion.

I wanted to be okay with horror, so I let myself experience tiny, homeopathic doses. I watched a TV special that showed a clip from the new film *Child's Play*. The doll made an angry face and that alone scared me. I watched another special that showed a clip from *Repo Man* in which a policeman opens the trunk of a car and is vaporized by whatever's inside. To this day it's one of my most vivid memories of anything I've seen on television.

When I was eight years old, I watched an episode of an anthology series called *Monsters*. In it, there was a beautiful girl who turned into a monster when somebody touched her. Her transformation scared the shit out of me. I left my room and found my parents. I told them about what I had watched as though I were confessing a crime.

Revisiting the episode now, a full three decades later, the shadows reveal themselves to be nothing to be afraid of. (The lead role was played by Soupy Sales, for crying out loud.) It's a silly episode, based entirely around the stock characters of the desperate traveling salesman and the lovelorn farmer's daughter. I'll give the show credit for the nice effect of the girl's face coming apart beneath the salesman's fingertips—precisely the moment that horrified me as a kid—but it quickly devolves into a farce in which a guy gets chased around a spooky house by monsters and eventually falls into a thresher.

As absurd as it feels to admit to having been haunted for so long by something I can now only see as ridiculous, it wasn't for want of trying. It's just that every time I attempted to engage with horror, every time I peeked through a crack in that door to prove to myself that I didn't have to be afraid, I failed. It beat me. Of course it did. That was the whole point of horror. I couldn't win.

Eventually, though, I finally went from being a kid who couldn't stand horror to an adult who loves it, who seeks out obscure titles to share with friends, who analyzes it and writes about it.

Resident Evil was that precise turning point for me. It was difficult, clunky, and impenetrable. It was confusing, badly acted, and totally unfair. It was a game I believed I'd never finish as long as I lived, and which I doubted anyone *could* finish. But it sucked me in.

I was responsible for Jill and Chris. I controlled them. I made their decisions. When I panicked, they panicked. When I got lost, they got lost. When I was attacked by a zombie, they bled out and died.

It was the first time I truly engaged with horror, let myself feel it on a deeper level, and confronted it.

Resident Evil felt like actual horror. Not a game with horror elements, but horror that happened to be a game. After playing it with Michael and Dave that first night, I laid in bed and mentally went over what I'd seen. I tried to figure out what the mysterious items we found could be used for. I wondered what the locked doors concealed. Would what I'd find empower me or kick the shit out of me? Would I be led closer to escape or deeper into danger? All these years later, I'm still analyzing *Resident Evil*, pulling it apart, being surprised by what I find hiding in the shadows.

It's something of a miracle to me that *Resident Evil* helped me reshape fear into fascination. That the game that had me panicking and running in circles now has me tracking down people around the world to share their memories of making it. The game that had me bracing myself during every loading screen, every change of camera angle, every time I heard the distant scuffling of an enemy I couldn't see, became my Rosetta Stone for understanding the language of horror itself.

Long after my interview with Charlie Kraslavsky, the original *Resident Evil* hero, I found an article in *Variety* about a potential reboot of the film franchise. My very first thought was to let him know.

"Holy shit!" he replied. "It's amazing how just verbalizing things occasionally causes them to manifest! I'm going to see if I can reach out to an agent and get representation ASAP, and have them contact the producer..."

I started this book with the intention of figuring out what horror was, how it worked, how it functioned, and why it endures… but at every turn, I found good people. Fun people. Sweet people. People happy to spend their time talking to me about a game they haven't thought about for decades. People who replied to my questions and requests for clarification when they no doubt had better things to do. People who, to be honest, didn't owe me the time of day.

Whatever horror is, for whatever reasons we love it, however it affects us, I've learned that it's great at bringing us together. Whether it was watching *Twilight Zone* reruns on New Year's Eve with my father, renting the worst movies imaginable with Michael, playing *AitD* with Art, laughing with strangers at *Night of the Living Dead*, talking about psychology with Kerr and Brown, or just bonding over *Resident Evil* with friends who found out I was working on this project and immediately began sharing their memories, horror—disgusting, dangerous, degenerate horror—brought us together. It's exactly like Brown told me: Experiencing horror with someone else gave me the chance to look at the person next to me on the couch, someone I trusted, and think, "I'm okay. I'm not really in danger."

At some point, deep into that first night, Michael removed the disc, packed up his PlayStation, and went back home. There was a finite number of times Michael, Dave, and I would get together to play video games. I guess we would have realized that if we'd thought about it, but so what? We were young. It was nothing to worry about. We had all the time in the world. Helicopter blades beating ceaselessly in the sky.

In my playthrough for this book, I finished *Resident Evil* with both other survivors in tow. In real life, I got out alone. I escaped New Jersey with nothing in my pockets and a car full of CDs. I had no job or place to live. I was terrified. I drove south until I hit Florida, at which point I stopped the car, rented a room, and had my CDs stolen as I slept.

But I survived. I grew up in a very poor town in which dealing drugs was by far the best way to make money. I grew up in an area that refused social progress, where gays and blacks weren't welcome. I got more than a few suspicious glances for reading books. I grew up with parents who were uncomfortable with and refused to acknowledge my mental health issues, leaving me to this day feeling stranded and ashamed. When I told them I struggled with serious depression and anxiety, they responded just as they had when they found out I needed glasses: They told me I was faking it. I was not able to see properly until I turned seventeen, got a job, saved my own money, and went to LensCrafters myself. Their insurance would have covered my glasses. Their insurance would have covered most of the things I needed.

I stopped speaking with Dave around the same time I left the state. He moved to California and started a family. I hope he's doing well. Michael did me a favor and removed himself from my life; he moved to Arizona to be with a girl I don't think I've ever met.

My own personal Wesker shoved me into the Spencer Mansion all those years ago. He knew what was inside. I didn't. He knew it would make me uncomfortable. He knew it would hurt. He knew there was no chance I'd find the exit.

And… well, he was right. But he didn't expect it to help me grow. He didn't expect me to figure out its traps and its methods. He didn't expect me to become so familiar with it over the years that I'd walk back inside, time and time again, of my own volition. Not as a victim but as a tourist.

It's nice to focus on monsters you know aren't real, to distract yourself from the real ones for a little while, from the ones you can't blast into a pile of smoked meat. It feels good to prove to yourself that you can survive. To remind yourself that you've survived already.

I got out the only way I could. Alone, desperate, my pockets empty. Whenever I do hear from old friends, stuck in that tiny town with nothing they're looking forward to, or whenever I find out that another person I went to school with died of an overdose, I experience a kind of survivor's guilt.

It's worth looking back, sometimes. It's worth reflecting, even if you wish you'd never been there in the first place. Even if it's all gone up in smoke. It's worth seeing how far you've come. It's worth reminding yourself that the odds were stacked against you, and they might always be, but you made it through. You'll see another day. And you'll be a little better prepared for whatever you find around the next corner.

ACKNOWLEDGEMENTS

I'D LIKE TO THANK THE LEGENDARY Lloyd Kaufman, who was kind enough to set time aside and write a foreword for a fan. He proved himself to be a sweet, supportive, remarkably friendly human being, and only about 80% as strange as I expected.

I'd like to thank everyone who made themselves available for an interview: Sharnay Brown, Margee Kerr, Barry Gjerde, Charlie Kraslavsky, Danelle Perry, Eric Pirius, Ward Sexton, and Greg Smith. I'd also like to thank expert fans Monique Alves and Fred Fouchet, who went out of their way to provide me with leads and information, as well as make me feel welcome in the community. Thanks as well to Jon Turner for pointing me in the direction of an obscure release of *Porco Rosso* containing the relevant English dub.

I'd like to thank Matthew Wong for rekindling my long-dormant interest in *Resident Evil*, and Matt Sainsbury, without whom I never would have pitched this thing in the first place. Thanks to Antonella Fratino,

Yuka Tokuyama, and Casey Roberson for translation and research assistance. Thanks also to Emily Suess, an excellent friend and an even better proofreader.

I'd like to thank Deb Gussman, Lisa Honaker, Tom Kinsella, GT Lenard, and Ken Tompkins, the esteemed literature professors at Stockton University who taught me to spend thousands of hours of my life analyzing every damned thing I encounter. I'd also like to thank the great poet Stephen Dunn.

I'd like to thank Peter Austin and Ben Potter from TripleJump, for being two of the most supportive, creative, and hilarious people I've ever had the sincere pleasure of working with. I'd also like to thank the great Adam Pacitti for providing me with that opportunity in the first place.

I'd like to thank Lauren Kimble, who has been there for me in ways no other human being has. I'd like to thank Shalini Basu for always encouraging me. I'd like to thank Jill Pintye, who sent me my first fan letter and made me believe I might actually amount to something. I'd like to thank my grandparents, Phil and Dolores, for being the family I needed.

I'd like to thank my important friend Jen Trynin, a musician whose incredible memoir *Everything I'm Cracked Up to Be* was more inspiring than she might have intended.

I'd like to thank Superorganism, whose self-titled debut I discovered at precisely the same time I started writing this book, and which remained in constant rotation all the way through.

I'd like to thank Gabe Durham and Michael P. Williams at Boss Fight Books. The former for his bottomless patience and the latter for his swift research and for keeping me sane throughout the writing process. Actually, mainly that. It was by far the bigger job.

Also on the Boss Fight Books side, many, many thanks to proofreaders Meghan Burklund, Matthew LeHew, Joseph M. Owens; to layout designers Christopher Moyer and Lori Colbeck; and to cover designer Cory Schmitz.

I'd also like to thank you, sincerely, for once again entering the world of survival horror with me.

NOTES

At Midnight I'll Take Your Soul

Metro.co.uk's David Jenkins spoke with Shinji Mikami in the June 24, 2014 feature "Shinji Mikami interview: the master of survival horror – 'I want to make a F1 game'": https://bit.ly/3a3QmoO.

William Audureau's interview with Mikami, "Shinji Mikami, «Resident Evil» et la source du jeu d'horreur," was published in Le Monde online on October 14, 2014 (https://bit.ly/2U2qG6u). Mikami speaks Japanese and the interview is in French. I've done my best to retain its spirit it in English.

Splatter University

For more differences between the Eastern and Western releases of the game (that is, *Biohazard* vs. *Resident Evil*), see the wiki entry at The Cutting Room Floor: https://bit.ly/2WstLhM.

Smile Before Death

H.P. Lovecraft's essay "Supernatural Horror in Literature" was first published in W. Paul Cook's one-shot magazine *The Recluse* (no. 1, 1927). For more information, see the essay's entry at the Internet Speculative Fiction Database (ISFDB): https://bit.ly/2QsS7V3.

Dogs of Hell

François Truffaut's book *Hitchcock* (also known as *Hitchcock/Truffaut*) was published in English by Simon and Schuster in 1967, with a revised edition in 1985. It was first released in French as *Le Cinéma selon Hitchcock* by Robert Laffont in 1966.

Them!

Interviews with the live-action cast were conducted via phone and email. Charlie Kraslavsky was interviewed via phone on May 12, 2018. Greg Smith was interviewed via phone on May 20, 2018. Eric Pirius was interviewed via email June 6, 2018.

All of Linda's comments in this chapter come from Fred Fouchet's interview at his gradually updating blog, Racoon STARS - The Resident Evil Live Actors (https://bit.ly/2x3r63v). Linda's comments were posted on March 8, 2019.

Trap Them and Kill Them

Robert M. Pirsig's book *Zen and the Art of Motorcycle Maintenance: An Inquiry into Values* was first published by William Morrow and Company in 1974.

Evidence for the real-life inspiration of Pirsig's "monkey trap" exists in literary sources such as Johann David Wyss's 1812 novel *Swiss Family Robinson* (as adapted into English by William Henry Giles Kingston), and an April 1876 article in *Frank Leslie's Popular Monthly* (vol. 1, no. 4) called "Monkey

Hunting" (https://bit.ly/2WBAkPp). Footage of a real monkey trap in action appears to be captured in the 1912 featurette "Hunting Monkeys," posted by Stephen Papworth to his YouTube channel: https://bit.ly/2WpihM1.

The Simpsons episode "Marge on the Lam" (season 5, episode 6) first aired on November 4, 1993.

All the Colors of the Dark

Christopher Buecheler's December 8, 2002 GameSpy article "Hall of Fame: Haunted House" provides a preliminary checklist of survival horror elements. It has been archived via WebCite here: https://bit.ly/33vKF0z.

Darren Grey's "Screw the Berlin Interpretation!" was published on his blog, Games of Grey, on May 14, 2013: https://bit.ly/2IYO8eM.

In the Mouth of Madness

Interviews with the voice cast were conducted via phone and email. Ward Sexton was interviewed on July 2, 2018, with follow-up questions answered via email. Barry Gjerde was interviewed via email February 1, 2019.

The Japan Airlines English-language dub of *Porco Rosso* was included as a foreign language audio track in a 2-disc Region 2 release of the film in Japan, distributed in 2002 by Buena Vista Home Entertainment as part of the "Ghibli Ippai Collection" series. For those trying to track down this release, it has the publisher number VWDZ-8022 and the Japanese article number (JAN) 4959241980229.

Barry Gjerde's interview with Monique Alves of Resident Evil Database was posted on September 30, 2015 in its original English and in Portuguese translation as "Entrevista | Barry Gjerde, dublador de Barry Burton no primeiro Resident Evil": https://bit.ly/3daDfnV.

Dean Harrington's interview with Welsh of Project Umbrella: The Resident Evil Compendium was published in August 2011 as "Dean Harrington Interview (Project Umbrella)": https://bit.ly/2IYqgb0.

I Eat Your Skin

Nikolai Gogol's 1835's short story "Diary of a Madman" (also known as "Memoirs of a Madman") was translated from Russian into English by Claud Field and released in the collection *The Mantle and Other Stories* (Frederick A. Stokes, 1916). A plain text version of this book is available through Project Gutenberg: https://bit.ly/2wjtwuQ.

Leigh Alexander reported on Frédéric Raynal's discussion of *AitD*'s logs at the 2012 Game Developers Conference in the March 9, 2012 Gamasutra article "GDC 2012: Inside the making of *Alone in the Dark*": https://bit.ly/2QpV3Sk

The Two Faces of Fear

Bill Demain reports on Stephen Spielberg and the making of Jaws in "How Malfunctioning Sharks Transformed the Movie Business," posted to Mental Floss on June 20, 2015: https://bit.ly/396gCgV.

Margee Kerr's *Scream: Chilling Adventures in the Science of Fear* was first published by PublicAffairs in 2015. A phone interview with Kerr for this book was conducted June 20, 2018.

A sit-down interview with psychologist Sharnay Brown for this book was conducted July 7, 2018.

It Follows

Capcom's press release for *Resident Evil*, "Horror Finds a New Home in Capcom's Resident Evil for the Sony PlayStation," was distributed on August 31, 1995 through Business Wire.

Douglas Imbrogno wrote about the *Resident Evil* press kit in "Giving a Video Game Company the Boot," published April 18, 1996 in *The Charleston Gazette*.

Tom Brown's baffling *Resident Evil/Sgt. Bilko* dual review was published under the title "Steve Martin, co-stars shine in hilarious 'Sgt. Bilko'" in the April 4, 1996 *The Times Recorder* of Zanesville, Ohio.

Roy Bassave's review of *Resident Evil* was widely published beyond the *Miami Herald*. The headline that went to print in the May 24, 1996 *Tallahassee Democrat* was "'Evil' oozes with action, bloody thrills: It's not a game for children.' The May 29 issue of the Moline, Illinois *Dispatch* got to the point: "Bloody 'Resident Evil' designed for adults."

Tom Ham's review of *Resident Evil* for the *Washington Post* was titled "Dead Residents," and was the feature review of the *Post*'s column "Buy it, Rent it, Forget it" on April 24, 1996.

Steve Marsh's review of *Nester's Funky Bowling* appeared in the same column as a lesser entry.

They Came from Within

Stephen King's *Danse Macabre* was first published by Everest House in 1981.

The Twilight Zone episode "The Monsters Are Due on Maple Street" (season 1, episode 22) first aired on March 4, 1960.

S.D. Perry's *The Umbrella Conspiracy* was first published by Pocket Books in 1998.

Fear No Evil

The first *Simpsons* Halloween special (featuring "The Raven" parody) was "Treehouse of Horror" (season 2, episode 3), and first aired October 25, 1990.

Margee Kerr's discussion with Jason Bailey was published as "The Psychology of Scary Movies" on October 27, 2016 at Flavorwire: https://bit.ly/2wbVWXM.

Reflections in Black

The episode of *Monsters* was "The Farmer's Daughter," which aired as season 2, episode 6 of the series on November 5, 1989.

A reboot of the Resident Evil film franchise was teased in John Hopewell's May 21, 2017 article "'Resident Evil' Franchise Set for a Reboot (EXCLUSIVE)" for Variety: https://bit.ly/2x474WK.

SPECIAL THANKS

For making our fifth season of books possible, Boss Fight Books would like to thank John Romero, Ian Chung, Fenric Cayne, Trey Adams, Jennifer Durham-Fowler, Cathy Durham & Ed Locke, Ken Durham & Nancy Magnusson Durham, Nate Mitchell, Lawliet Tamaki Aivazis, Cassandra Newman, seanz0r, Zach Davis, Andrew "Xestrix" Carlson, Ant'ny Fataski, David Goodenough, Adam Hejmowski, Joshua Mallory, and Sean 'Ariamaki' Riedinger.

ALSO FROM
BOSS FIGHT BOOKS